MAXnotes

William Shakespeare's

King Lear

Text by
Corinna Siebert Ruth
(M.A., California State University-Fresno)
Department of English
Fresno Pacific College
Fresno, California

Illustrations by
Karen Pica

 Research & Education Association

MAXnotes® for
KING LEAR

Printed in the United States of America

Library of Congress Catalog Card Number 98-66193

International Standard Book Number 0-87891-989-9

What **MAXnotes®** *Will Do for You*

This book is intended to help you absorb the essential contents and features of William Shakespeare's *King Lear* and to help you gain a thorough understanding of the work. Our book has been designed to do this more quickly and effectively than any other study guide.

For best results, this **MAXnotes** book should be used as a companion to the actual work, not instead of it. The interaction between the two will greatly benefit you.

To help you in your studies, this book presents the most up-to-date interpretations of every section of the actual work, followed by questions and fully explained answers that will enable you to analyze the material critically. The questions also will help you to test your understanding of the work and will prepare you for discussions and exams.

Meaningful illustrations are included to further enhance your understanding and enjoyment of the literary work. The illustrations are designed to place you into the mood and spirit of the work's settings.

The **MAXnotes** also include summaries, character lists, explanations of plot, and chapter-by-chapter analyses. A biography of the author and discussion of the work's historical context will help you put this literary piece into the proper perspective of what is taking place.

The use of this study guide will save you the hours of preparation time that would ordinarily be required to arrive at a complete grasp of this work of literature. You will be well-prepared for classroom discussions, homework, and exams. The guidelines that are included for writing papers and reports on various topics will prepare you for any added work which may be assigned.

The **MAXnotes** will take your grades "to the max."

Dr. Max Fogiel
Program Director

Contents

Section One: *Introduction* 1
    The Life and Work of William Shakespeare 1
    Historical Background 3
    Master List of Characters 4
    Summary of the Play 5
    Estimated Reading Time 6

Each scene includes List of Characters, Summary, Analysis, Study Questions and Answers, and Suggested Essay Topics.

Section Two: *Act I* 7
    Scene 1 7
    Scene 2 15
    Scene 3 20
    Scene 4 23
    Scene 5 29

Section Three: *Act II* 33
    Scene 1 33
    Scenes 2 and 3 37
    Scene 4 42

Section Four: *Act III* 49
    Scene 1 49
    Scene 2 52
    Scene 3 57
    Scene 4 60
    Scene 5 65
    Scene 6 68
    Scene 7 72

Section Five: *Act IV* 79
    Scene 1 79
    Scene 2 83
    Scene 3 88
    Scene 4 91

Scene 5 95
Scene 6 98
Scene 7 107

Section Six: *Act V* 113
Scene 1 and 2 113
Scene 3 119

Section Seven: *Sample Analytical Papers* 130

Section Eight: *Bibliography* 137

MAXnotes® are simply the best – but don't just take our word for it...

"... I have told every bookstore in the area to carry your MAXnotes. They are the only notes I recommend to my students. There is no comparison between MAXnotes and all other notes ..."
    – High School Teacher & Reading Specialist, Arlington High School, Arlington, MA

"... I discovered the MAXnotes when a friend loaned me her copy of the MAXnotes for Romeo and Juliet. The book really helped me understand the story. Please send me a list of stores in my area that carry the MAXnotes. I would like to use more of them ..."
    – Student, San Marino, CA

"... The two MAXnotes titles that I have used have been very, very, useful in helping me understand the subject matter reviewed. Thank you for creating the MAXnotes series ..."
    – Student, Morrisville, PA

A Glance at Some of the Characters

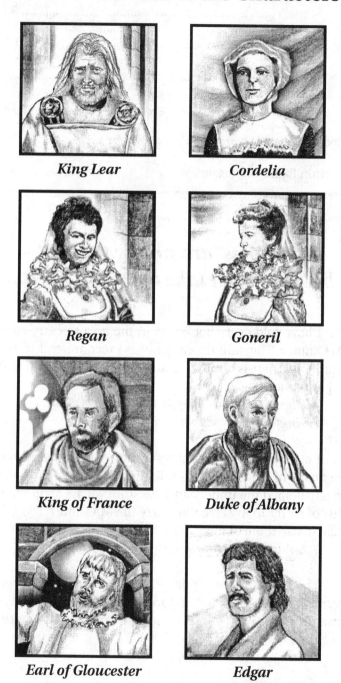

King Lear

Cordelia

Regan

Goneril

King of France

Duke of Albany

Earl of Gloucester

Edgar

SECTION ONE

Introduction

The Life and Work of William Shakespeare

Details about William Shakespeare's life are sketchy, mostly mere surmise based upon court or other clerical records. His parents, John and Mary (Arden), were married about 1557; she was of the landed gentry, and he a yeoman—a glover and commodities merchant. By 1568, John had risen through the ranks of town government and held the position of high bailiff, similar to mayor. William, the eldest son and the third of eight children, was born in 1564, probably on April 23, several days before his baptism on April 26 in Stratford-upon-Avon. Shakespeare is also believed to have died on the same date—April 23—in 1611.

It is believed William attended the local grammar school in Stratford where his parents lived, and studied primarily Latin rhetoric, logic, and literature. Shakespeare probably left school at age 15, which was the norm, to take a job, especially since this was the period of his father's financial difficulty. At age 18 (1582), William married Anne Hathaway, a local farmer's daughter who was eight years his senior. Their first daughter (Susanna) was born six months later (1583), and twins Judith and Hamnet were born in 1585.

Shakespeare's life can be divided into three periods: the first 20 years in Stratford, which include his schooling, early marriage, and fatherhood; the next 25 years as an actor and playwright in London; and the last five in retirement back in Stratford where he enjoyed moderate wealth gained from his theatrical successes. The years linking the first two periods are marked by a lack of information about Shakespeare, and are often referred to as the "dark years."

At some point during the "dark years," Shakespeare began his career with a London theatrical company, perhaps in 1589, for he was already an actor and playwright of some note by 1592. Shakespeare apparently wrote and acted for numerous theatrical companies, including Pembroke's Men, and Strange's Men, which later became the Chamberlain's Men, with whom he remained for the rest of his career.

In 1592, the Plague closed the theaters for about two years, and Shakespeare turned to writing book length narrative poetry. Most notable were "Venus and Adonis" and "The Rape of Lucrece," both of which were dedicated to the Earl of Southampton, whom scholars accept as Shakespeare's friend and benefactor despite a lack of documentation. During this same period, Shakespeare was writing his sonnets, which are more likely signs of the time's fashion rather than actual love poems detailing any particular relationship. He returned to playwriting when theaters reopened in 1594, and did not continue to write poetry. His sonnets were published without his consent in 1609, shortly before his retirement.

Amid all of his success, Shakespeare suffered the loss of his only son, Hamnet, who died in 1596 at the age of 11. But Shakespeare's career continued unabated, and in London in 1599, he became one of the partners in the new Globe Theater, which was built by the Chamberlain's Men.

Shakespeare wrote very little after 1612, which was the year he completed *Henry VIII*. It was during a performance of this play in 1613 that the Globe caught fire and burned to the ground. Sometime between 1610 and 1613, Shakespeare returned to Stratford, where he owned a large house and property, to spend his remaining years with his family.

William Shakespeare died on April 23, 1616, and was buried two days later in the chancel of Holy Trinity Church where he had been baptized exactly 52 years earlier. His literary legacy included 37 plays, 154 sonnets and five major poems.

Incredibly, most of Shakespeare's plays had never been published in anything except pamphlet form, and were simply extant as acting scripts stored at the Globe. Theater scripts were not regarded as literary works of art, but only the basis for the performance. Plays were simply a popular form of entertainment for all layers of society in Shakespeare's time. Only the efforts of two of Shakespeare's company, John Heminges and Henry Condell, preserved his 36 plays (minus *Pericles*, the thirty-seventh).

Historical Background

Shakespeare's work can be understood more clearly if we follow its development as a reflection of the rapidly-changing world of the sixteenth and early seventeenth centuries in which he lived. After the colorful reign of Henry VIII, which ushered in the Protestant Reformation, England was never the same. The contributions of John Calvin and Michelangelo (who both died the year Shakespeare was born) had a decisive role in the European Reformation and the Renaissance. When Queen Elizabeth I came to the throne in 1558, the time was right to bring in "the golden age" of English history. The arts flourished during the Elizabethan era. Some of Shakespeare's contemporary dramatists were such notables as Christopher Marlowe and Ben Jonson.

King James VI of Scotland succeeded Elizabeth to the throne after her death in 1603, uniting the kingdoms of England and Scotland. The monarch's new title was King James I. Fortunately for Shakespeare, the new king was a patron of the arts and agreed to sponsor the King's Men, Shakespeare's theatrical group, named in the King's honor. According to the *Stationers' Register* recorded on November 26, 1607, *King Lear* was performed for King James I at Whitehall on St. Stephen's night as a Christmas celebration on December 26, 1606.

The legend of King Lear, well-known in Shakespeare's day, was about a mythical British king dating back to the obscurity of ancient times. It was first recorded in 1135 by Geoffrey of Monmouth in *Historia Britonum*. In 1574 it appeared in *A Mirror for Magistrates* and later in Holinshed's *Chronicles* in 1577. The subplot, which concerned Gloucester and his sons, was taken from Philip Sidney's *Arcadia*. An older version of the play called *The True Chronicle History of King Leir* first appeared on the stage in 1590. Comments on public response to the play in Shakespeare's day would necessarily be based on conjecture, but in 1681, an adaptation of the original play was published by Nahum Tate, a dramatist of the Restoration period. Tate's sentimental adaptation gives the play a happy ending in which Lear and Gloucester are united with their children. Virtue is rewarded and justice reigns in Tate's version. It was not until 1838 that Macready reinstated Shakespeare's original version on the stage.

Major Characters

Lear, King of Britain—A mythical king of pre-Christian Britain, well-known in the folklore of Shakespeare's day. Lear is a foolish king who intends to divide his kingdom among his three daughters.

Cordelia—Lear's youngest daughter who speaks the truth.

The King of France and the Duke of Burgundy—They are both Cordelia's suitors, but the King of France marries her.

Regan and Goneril—Lear's selfish daughters who flatter him in order to gain his wealth and power.

Duke of Albany—Goneril's husband whose sympathy for Lear turns him against his wife.

Duke of Cornwall—Regan's husband who joins his wife in her devious scheme to destroy King Lear and usurp his power.

Earl of Gloucester—In the subplot, Gloucester's afflictions with his sons parallel those of Lear's with his daughters.

Edgar—The legitimate son of Gloucester.

Edmund—The illegitimate son of Gloucester who stops at nothing to gain power.

Earl of Kent—Kent is banished by King Lear for trying to intervene when Lear disinherits Cordelia.

Fool—The King's professional court jester whose witty and prophetic remarks are a wise commentary on Lear's shortsightedness.

Oswald—Goneril's steward who attempts to kill Gloucester.

Summary of the Play

From the legendary story of King Lear, Shakespeare presents a dramatic version of the relationships between parents and their children. Lear, king of ancient Britain, decides to divide his kingdom among his three daughters: Goneril and Regan, the wives of the Duke of Albany and the Duke of Cornwall, and Cordelia, his youngest and favorite. In an attempt to give the "largest bounty" to the one who loves him most, the king asks for his daughters' expressions of affection. He receives embellished speeches of endearment from the older two, but Cordelia modestly speaks the truth, angering her father, who disinherits her and banishes her forever. Trying to intercede on Cordelia's behalf, the Earl of Kent is also banished. The King of France marries Lear's dowerless daughter. Meanwhile, the Earl of Gloucester is deceived by his illegitimate son, Edmund, who leads him to believe that Edgar, the earl's legitimate son, is plotting to murder his father.

Lear's plans to live with his two older daughters are immediately thwarted when Goneril turns on him, reducing his train of followers by half. In shock from her ingratitude, Lear decides to seek refuge with Regan. Instead of admonishing her sister for her actions as Lear expects, Regan is harsh with him, suggesting that he apologize to Goneril. Heartbroken and rejected, Lear totters out into the storm with only his Fool and Kent to keep him company. Kent, who is now in disguise, finds refuge in a hovel for the king, who has been driven mad by his suffering. There they meet Edgar, disguised as Tom o'Bedlam, hiding in fear for his life. Gloucester soon arrives and hurries Lear off to Dover, where Cordelia is waiting with a French army ready to restore her father's kingdom. Cordelia cares for her father in the camp, and their severed relationship is restored.

In the meantime, Cornwall gouges out Gloucester's eyes, calling him a traitor. Still in disguise, Edgar leads his blind father to Dover. Edmund, in command of the English army, defeats the French, taking Cordelia and Lear as prisoners. As Gloucester is dying, Edgar reveals his true identity to his father. Edgar kills Edmund, but cannot save Cordelia whom Edmund has ordered to be hanged. Lear dies, grief-stricken over Cordelia's death. Rivalry over their love for Edmund leads Goneril to poison Regan and then stab herself. Albany, Kent, and Edgar are left to restore some semblance of order to the kingdom.

Estimated Reading Time

Shakespeare's poetic drama, written to be viewed by an audience, usually takes approximately three hours to perform on the stage. It would be possible to read it almost as fast the first time around to get the plot of the story. An auditory tape of *King Lear*, available at most university or county libraries, is an excellent device that can be used to follow along with the text, making the drama more interesting by bringing the characters alive. After the initial reading, however, it should be read more carefully, taking special note of the difficult words and phrases that are glossed at the bottom of most Shakespearean texts. This reading would probably take about six hours for the entire play, allowing a little more than an hour for each of the five acts. Since the acts of *King Lear* vary from three to seven scenes each, the length of reading time for each act will, of course, vary.

Act I

Act I, Scene 1

New Characters:

King Lear: *king of pre-Christian Britain; protagonist of the play*

Goneril: *King Lear's oldest daughter with whom he lives first*

Regan: *King Lear's middle daughter who refuses to take him in*

Cordelia: *King Lear's youngest daughter who is banished and disinherited*

Duke of Cornwall: *husband of Regan who stops at nothing to gain power*

Duke of Albany: *the mild-mannered husband of Goneril*

Earl of Kent: *King Lear's devoted courtier who is banished*

Earl of Gloucester: *protagonist of the subplot whose family situation is analogous to Lear's*

Edmund: *bastard son of Gloucester*

King of France: *marries Cordelia without a dowry*

Duke of Burgundy: *Cordelia's suitor who rejects Lear's dowerless daughter*

Summary

Setting the scene for King Lear's rumored intention of dividing his kingdom, Gloucester and Kent discuss the King's preference between his sons-in-law, the Duke of Albany and the Duke of Cornwall. Kent is introduced to Edmund, Gloucester's illegitimate son, whom his father loves no less than his legitimate son, Edgar.

The trumpet sounds and King Lear and his attendants enter with his two sons-in-law and his three daughters: Goneril, Regan, and Cordelia. He immediately orders Gloucester to attend to the King of France and the Duke of Burgundy who are both suitors contending for Cordelia's hand in marriage. Gloucester leaves and without delay Lear clarifies his intended purpose. He plans to divide his kingdom among his three daughters, giving the greatest share to the daughter who publicly professes to love him most.

Goneril, Lear's oldest daughter, is called on first. She flatters her father into believing that she loves him more than "words can wield the matter." Not to be outdone, Regan claims to love the King as much as her sister does, except that Goneril "comes too short." Expecting a grander expression of love from Cordelia, his favorite, the King is surprised and angry when her reply is simply "Nothing, my lord." He implores her to "mend [her] speech a little" or else she "may mar [her] fortunes." She tries to explain to the King that she only speaks the truth, but it is to no avail. Lear banishes her without an inheritance or a dowry.

In a futile attempt to change the King's mind, Kent argues on Cordelia's behalf but is also banished. He bids goodbye to the King, commending Cordelia for speaking truthfully and admonishing Goneril and Regan to live up to their "large speeches" of love for their father.

Gloucester ushers in the King of France and the Duke of Burgundy. They are both made aware of Cordelia's banishment and recent loss of fortune and are given a chance to accept her without a dowry. The King of France is confused, wondering what Cordelia, who had always had been Lear's favorite, could have done to deserve such treatment from her father. Cordelia begs her father to understand that she lacks the "glib and oily art" to speak of her love for him, but he only responds with a wish that she had never been born. Burgundy appeals to Lear to change his mind about the inheritance, but the King is unyielding. When Burgundy rejects Cordelia for lack of a dowry, she responds with a refusal to marry him if he is only interested in her "fortune." The King of France who has gained a new admiration and respect for Cordelia, happily accepts King Lear's "dow'rless daughter" and offers to make her the new Queen of France.

Without her father's blessing, Cordelia bids farewell to her sisters with tearstained eyes, telling them that she wishes she could leave her father in better hands. Goneril and Regan sneer at her request for them to love Lear well. When they are alone together, the older sisters quickly turn on their father, discussing his "poor judgment" and making plans to usurp his power to prevent any more of his rash behavior.

Analysis

The universality of *King Lear* revolves around the theme of appearances versus reality as it relates to the world of filial love and, in Lear's case, ingratitude. In the opening scene we see Lear as a monarch commanding respect and love from his daughters. Lear speaks in the language of the "royal we," which was language given to the nobility in Shakespeare's plays. "Which of you shall we say doth love us most,/ That we our largest bounty may extend." In his illusory world, he mistakes the flattery of Goneril and Regan as the truth and interprets Cordelia's plain speech as a lack of love for her father. Lear completely misses the point of Cordelia's words, which show her love to be "more ponderous" than her tongue. In his selfish attempt to buy his daughters' love with material possessions, however, he is blind to the fact that one cannot manipulate true affection.

Images of Lear's blindness or lack of insight are revealed when Kent coaxes him to "See better, Lear" or when Goneril claims that she loves her father "dearer than eyesight." Unaware of what he is relinquishing to his older daughters, Lear's illusions carry him even further when he hopes to "retain/ The name (king), and all th' addition to the king." He expects to keep his title and all the honors and official privileges and powers inherent in that title. The folly of that illusion will later haunt him as he is driven out to face the reality of the storm with only his Fool to keep him company.

Some critics have censured Cordelia's unbending attitude toward the King in the first scene as evidence of her pride. In allowing Cordelia the "asides" to express her repulsion for her sisters' flowery speeches, however, Shakespeare characterizes her as a completely honest person who acts as a foil to Goneril and Regan. Cordelia's response, "Nothing," and Lear's subsequent repetition of the word, punctuate Aristotle's idea that "Nothing will come of nothing." Ironically, these words, spoken by Lear himself, foreshadow the move from order to chaos throughout the rest of the drama. In the eyes of the King of France, Cordelia is, paradoxically, "most rich being poor." France extols her virtues and acknowledges her loss by promising to make it up to her as his queen.

Lear, in his ill-considered haste, banishes both Cordelia and Kent for speaking the truth. Kent feels duty-bound to stop Lear's rash behavior. "When Lear is mad./ ...Think'st thou that duty shall have dread to speak/ When power to flattery bows?" Kent alludes to Lear's "madness," which will dominate the action in subsequent scenes of the play.

Writing in the consciousness of his own age, Shakespeare's view of the natural order of things was still heavily influenced by the recent ideas of the Middle Ages. Lear refuses to accept Cordelia's love when it is given only "According to my bond." He fails to abide by her natural allegiance to her king and father and casts her out, thereby, destroying the natural order based on the hierarchy of all beings and things, animate and inanimate. Although this concept of the "chain of being" had its genesis with Plato and Aristotle, it was central to Medieval thought and did, in fact, stretch far beyond. In the seventeenth century, Leibniz writes about it; and as late as the eighteenth century, Alexander Pope explicitly describes the hierarchy and possible destruction of the natural order.

> Vast chain of being! which from God began,
> Natures aethereal, human, angel, man,
> Beast, bird, fish, insect, what no eye can see,...
> Where, one step broken, the great scale's destroyed...

Shakespeare sets the scene for this disorder in the opening lines of the play. The prose dialogue of Kent and Gloucester discussing the bastardy and illegitimacy of Edmund with a flippant attitude is unnatural for Gloucester's station in life. Kent also joins

him with an attitude of acceptance unable to "smell a fault." To make matters worse, Gloucester has a legitimate son whom he loves equally as well. This equality, seeming correct and natural in our modern times, would have been unnatural and shocking in Elizabethan England. It is significant that they both speak in prose rather than verse, since prose is usually set aside for servants and other lowly characters speaking in the colloquial language of the day. Shakespeare often uses prose, however, for humorously coarse or bawdy conversation that does, perhaps, not warrant the use of verse. Later, all three of the characters will speak in blank verse, unrhymed iambic pentameter (10 syllables to a line with the accent on every second syllable), which is befitting their social rank. Gloucester and his sons, Edmund and Edgar are the main characters involved in the subplot of the play, which commences in the next scene.

Study Questions

1. Explain briefly why King Lear has called his family together in the first scene.

2. Which characters are involved in the subplot of the story?

3. Name one of the major themes of the play.

4. At what period in history does the play take place?

5. Why does Kent defend Cordelia when her father banishes her?

6. Why does the Duke of Burgundy reject the offer of Cordelia's hand in marriage?

7. Who are the Duke of Albany and the Duke of Cornwall?

8. Who eventually marries Lear's dowerless daughter? Where will she live after her marriage?

9. What advice does Cordelia give to her sisters as she leaves with the King of France?

10. What do Goneril and Regan do as soon as everyone is gone and they are alone together?

Answers

1. King Lear calls his family together in order to divide his kingdom among his three daughters.

2. Gloucester, his illegitimate son Edmund, and his legitimate son Edgar, are the characters involved in the subplot.

3. A major theme of the play is appearance versus reality. King Lear is more impressed with his older daughters' flowery speeches of love than Cordelia's sincere response.

4. The play supposedly takes place in pre-Christian Britain but exhibits many sixteenth-century values.

5. Kent defends Cordelia because he feels it is his duty to keep the King from making a "rash" decision.

6. The Duke of Burgundy will not accept Cordelia because she has no dowry to bring into the marriage.

7. The Duke of Albany is Goneril's husband, and the Duke of Cornwall is Regan's husband.

8. The King of France marries Cordelia in spite of her banishment and lack of a dowry. He will take her to France.

9. Cordelia asks her sisters to treat their father well.

10. Goneril and Regan immediately begin to plot ways in which to usurp the power of the King, their father.

Suggested Essay Topics

1. In the play, King Lear requests his daughters' public profession of love to him. Cordelia is often criticized for being too proud to give her father the response he wants to hear. Analyze the incident where Cordelia responds with "Nothing, my Lord." Discuss her obedience to her father as it relates to the philosophy of the hierarchy of all beings. Support your answer with examples from the play.

2. Goneril and Regan both please King Lear with flowery speeches of love and devotion to him. Compare and contrast their attitudes before the division of the kingdom with

their attitudes at the end of Scene 1. Are they completely evil? Do they show some signs of rational thought regarding the King's future? Cite examples from the play to support your answer.

Act I, Scene 2

Summary

In Edmund's opening soliloquy, we move from King Lear's palace in the previous scene to the castle of the Earl of Gloucester. The subplot of the play is set in motion when Edmund calls upon his goddess, Nature, to whose law he is bound. As the illegitimate son of Gloucester, Edmund challenges his supposed inferiority to his brother Edgar. He is also aware that Edgar is no dearer to his father than he is and intends to capitalize on the Earl's trust in him. Determined to snatch his half-brother's land and future title as Earl of Gloucester, Edmund forges his brother's name in a letter in which Edgar presumably suggests a plan to murder his father. With the letter in his hand, Edmund confidently invokes the gods to "stand up for bastards" as he prepares to meet his father.

As Gloucester enters, he is preoccupied with the disturbing events of the recent past. Edmund, however, makes sure that his father sees him attempting to hide the letter. Gloucester's curiosity is aroused by Edmund's strange behavior, and he repeatedly questions him about the piece of paper in his hand. Edmund, pretending to spare his father's feelings, cautiously breaks the news. He tells him the letter is from his brother, and says "I find it not fit for your o'erlooking." This only increases Gloucester's curiosity, and, after much coaxing, Edmund finally hands it to him. Gloucester, stunned by its contents, questions the handwriting but is easily convinced it is Edgar's. Gloucester's harsh invectives against Edgar, the seeming villain, are promptly checked by Edmund, however. Under the guise of protecting his father's safety, Edmund asks him to leave the matter to him.

In the meantime, Gloucester blames the "late eclipses in the sun and moon" for the recent happenings turning son against father and the king against child. When his father is out of sight,

Edmund ridicules his superstitious beliefs, convinced that people blame the stars as an excuse for their own faults.

When Edgar approaches, Edmund feigns an interest in astrology, much to his brother's surprise. Quickly changing the subject, however, Edmund moves to the matter at hand, which is to inform his brother that their father is furiously angry at Edgar for some unknown reason. He advises Edgar to arm himself if he plans to go out in public and gives him a key to his lodgings, where he will be safe until a proper time when Edmund will bring Edgar to their father.

After Edgar leaves, Edmund, realizing he has easily duped his father and brother, revels over their gullibility.

Analysis

Edmund's soliloquy, introducing the subplot of the play, reveals an attitude of free will and equality that is easily understood by people in modern society. Our sympathies are certainly with Edmund in his complaint: "Wherefore should I/ Stand in the plague of custom." He pierces our sensibilities with his satirical repetition of the word "legitimate," and the sensation is heightened further with his alliterative "Why brand they us/ With base? with baseness? bastardy? base, base?" Today, in all fairness, we would agree that people are not "base" by virtue of their birth. Reference to legitimate and illegitimate children is seldom seen in today's world. But we must be careful not to mistake Edmund's view as an ideal of modern society. The goddess Nature that Edgar invokes has no righteousness. There is, instead, a devil-may-care attitude where "gods stand up for bastards" regardless of what they do. Edmund's actions are brought about by deception, linking him with the evils of Goneril and Regan as the play progresses. He judges his superiority "by the lusty stealth of nature" in which he has "more composition" than the "dull, stale, tired bed" of marriage. Edmund's idea of Nature is based mostly on matter and animal appetites. Instead of harmony and order in the universe, his law of nature brings chaos and death.

Edmund's response to Gloucester's question concerning the paper he was reading is "Nothing, my lord." It is significant that these same words, spoken by Cordelia, started the action involving Lear's lack of insight, which resulted in her banishment. Gloucester also lacks insight to make good choices concerning Edgar. In his hasty judgment of him, he is immediately gulled into seeing him as a "brutish villain." Shakespeare's use of images pertaining to sight has a symbolic significance in this scene. When Gloucester begs, "Let's see, let's see," he does, in fact, lack the insight to see the truth, just as he does when he says, "Come, if it be nothing, I shall not need spectacles." But spectacles do not give him insight, and, consequently, his poor judgment of Edgar parallels Lear's judgment of Cordelia.

Gloucester's view of life in his speech beginning with "These late eclipses in the sun and moon" is seen by Edmund as superstition or an evasive way of blaming the stars or the heavens for his faults. Again, Edmund presents a rebuttal that appeals to our modern sensibilities. At the heart of the matter, however, lies his view of nature as a morally indifferent world that is simply a force with which to be reckoned. In contrast, Gloucester's view of nature reflects the hierarchy of all beings. When son turns against father or father against child, that hierarchy is disturbed and "all ruinous disorders follow us disquietly to our graves." Some critics believe that Edmund's view of nature was a new concept—just beginning to take hold in the sixteenth century—that was radically opposed to the orthodox traditions. Nevertheless, Lear, Gloucester, and Kent will see the relationship between the heavenly bodies and their effect on the lives of people throughout the drama.

Study Questions

1. In his soliloquy, what does Edmund want to take from his half-brother Edgar?

2. What is the piece of paper Edmund is supposedly hiding from his father? What does it say?

3. What is Gloucester's reaction to the letter?

4. Give an example of alliteration in Edmund's soliloquy.

5. What does Edmund think of his father's view of nature?

6. What does Edmund tell Edgar about his father?

7. What does Edmund tell Edgar he must do if he intends to

walk in public?

8. Where is Edgar instructed to go?

9. How will Edgar be able to talk to his father?

10. Why is Edmund gloating at the end of the scene?

Answers

1. Edmund wants to take land that now rightfully belongs to his half-brother Edgar.

2. The piece of paper is a forged letter supposedly written by Edgar plotting his father's murder.

3. Gloucester's reaction to the letter sends him into a rage against his son Edgar.

4. An example of alliteration in Edmund's soliloquy is "With base? with baseness? bastardy? base, base?"

5. Edmund thinks his father is only blaming the stars for his own failures.

6. Edmund tells Edgar his father is very angry with him and might harm him.

7. Edmund tells Edgar he must arm himself if he intends to "stir abroad."

8. Edgar is instructed to go to Edmund's lodging.

9. Edmund promises to bring Edgar to his father so he can hear him speak.

10. Edmund gloats because he has duped his father and half-brother into believing his story.

Suggested Essay Topics

1. In his soliloquy, Edmund addresses issues of equality and free will. Analyze these issues in the light of our modern-day society. Do you agree with Edmund? Do you disagree? Did Edmund present a law of nature with harmony and order? Use examples from the play to support your answer.

2. Act I, Scene 2 starts the action of the subplot of *King Lear*. Explain the subplot and tell how it parallels the main plot of the play. Describe the characters in the subplot and tell who they are analogous to in the main plot, giving examples from the play to support your answer.

Act I, Scene 3

New Character:

Oswald: *Goneril's steward who willingly carries out the evil schemes of his mistress*

Summary

This scene is set in the Duke of Albany's palace, the home of Lear's oldest daughter Goneril with whom he has been living since the division of the kingdom. Goneril questions her steward, Oswald, and finds that her father has struck her gentleman for chiding his Fool. She is distraught over the King's behavior, claiming that he "upbraids us/ On every trifle." She says too that his knights "grow riotous." She is, in fact, so angry at her father that she does not want to speak to him and instructs Oswald to tell the King she is sick when he comes back from his hunting trip. In retaliation for her father's behavior, she also gives Oswald a directive to cut back on his usual services to the King. She will answer for it later if he gives Oswald any trouble.

Horns sound as Lear and his entourage return from their hunting trip. Goneril hastily directs Oswald to treat the King with "weary negligence" and instruct the servants under his command to do the same. If her father does not like it, she says, he can go live with her sister Regan. Goneril is well aware that she and Regan are of like mind concerning their father. She calls him foolish for trying to cling to his power and authority after he has officially relinquished it.

Goneril continues to rail bitterly against her father, calling him an old fool who needs to be treated like a baby again. He needs "flatteries" but also "checks" or reprimands. Hastily, she tells Oswald to instruct his knights to greet Lear with cold looks. With that, she hurries off to write to Regan informing her of what has transpired.

Analysis

This short scene acts as an interlude between the introduction of the subplot and Lear's dialogue with the disguised Kent. As background for the subsequent action of the play, the scene gives us our first brief glimpse of the signs of deterioration of the father/daughter relationship. It comes as no surprise, however, since we have been forewarned of the intentions of Goneril and Regan at the end of the first act.

Goneril repeatedly insists on blaming Lear's actions on "the infirmity of his age." It should be noted, however, that he has just returned from a strenuous hunting expedition which seems to be quite a feat for an "idle old man." In her eagerness to strip him of his power, Goneril deceives even herself. Her obvious disrespect for her father validates Cordelia's perceptive honesty in Act I when she says, "I know you what you are." Goneril's actions toward her father would have been seen as a clear violation of the natural hierarchy by the Elizabethan audience of Shakespeare's day.

Study Questions

1. Where is the scene set?

2. What arrangement have Goneril and Regan made for the care of their father, the king?

3. Where has King Lear gone at the beginning of the scene?

4. What kind of servant is Oswald?

5. What does Goneril instruct Oswald to do in order to anger the king?

6. Why does Goneril pretend to be sick?

7. Where does Goneril plan to tell her father to go if he does not like it at her palace?

8. Why does Goneril decide to write to her sister?

9. What is the significance of the father/daughter relationship in this scene?

10. What would an Elizabethan audience of Shakespeare's day have thought of Goneril's attitude toward her father?

Answers

1. It is set in the palace of the Duke of Albany.

2. Goneril will keep her father first. Then she and Regan will alternate each month.

3. The King has gone hunting.

4. Oswald is a steward in charge of other servants.

5. Goneril instructs Oswald and his fellows to treat Lear's knights with cold looks and to put on "weary negligence."

6. Goneril is too angry to speak to her father when he comes home from his hunting trip.

7. Goneril will tell Lear to go live with her sister Regan.

8. Goneril hastily writes to her sister to tell her that Lear is acting badly and might decide to come live with her.

9. This is our first glimpse of the deterioration of the father/daughter relationship.

10. They would have seen Goneril's attitude as a violation of the natural hierarchy.

Suggested Essay Topics

1. Act I, Scene 3 is a short scene, but it is essential to the understanding of the play. Explain what purpose it serves. Why are Goneril's speeches important? In what way does the scene help to clarify the deterioration of relationships? Explain your answer.

2. The theme of old age is at the heart of Goneril's attitude toward her father. Discuss Goneril's attitude toward old people in general. How does she view their worth? Cite examples from the play to support your answer.

Act I, Scene 4

New Characters:

Knight: *one of Lear's many attendants*

Fool: *the king's court jester*

Summary

The scene continues in Albany's palace, where Kent is considering the success of his disguise. He is convinced that if he falsifies his accent, the masquerade will be complete. Ironically, he wishes to remain loyal to the King who has banished him. Just as Lear returns from his hunting trip, Kent appears disguised in servant's garb. Lear questions his abilities and his motives for wanting to serve him. Answering each question in a jovial manner, Kent portrays a character unlike his own. Convinced of Kent's qualifications, Lear invites him to join him as his servant and immediately calls for his dinner and his Fool.

Oswald, Goneril's steward, enters and Lear demands to see his daughter. Walking away, Oswald purposely ignores the King's request. Lear calls him back, but when Oswald does not respond, he sends his knight after him. The knight comes back with the news that Oswald rudely refused to obey the King. Shocked at such defiance, Lear discusses the matter with his knight, who has also noticed the recent "abatement of kindness" evident in the servants, Goneril, and the Duke of Albany. Lear again calls for his Fool, whom he has not seen for two weeks and is told that he has been pining away for Cordelia ever since she left for France. Unwilling to discuss it further, Lear quickly dismisses the idea, instructing his knight to bring Goneril and his Fool to him.

In the meantime, Oswald appears and addresses Lear with insolence and disrespect. Lear strikes him and Kent trips his heels and pushes him out. Grateful to Kent, the King hands him money for his service.

Lear's Fool finally appears with humorous and witty remarks about his coxcomb or cap. The Fool's satiric jesting about Lear's loss of his title and the division of his kingdom is a sad but honest

commentary on his plight in which his "daughters" have become his "mothers." Goneril enters and the King kindly asks her why she wears a frown on her face. The Fool chastises him for patronizing her. Goneril confronts her father with a long diatribe concerning his quarreling and riotous servants. She blames him for allowing them to exhibit this kind of behavior. Lear cannot believe these words are coming from his own daughter. Goneril is relentless, however, finally demanding that he diminish his "train of servants" so that there will be order in the palace again, and he will be able to act in a manner befitting his age. Lear reacts with rage, calling her a "degenerate bastard" and promising to trouble her no longer.

Unaware of the situation, Albany enters, telling Lear to be patient, but he turns a deaf ear to his son-in-law. Claiming his "train are men of choice," he tells Goneril she is lying about their conduct. Cordelia's faults suddenly seem small compared to Goneril's, and he beats his head, blaming himself for his foolishness and poor judgment in giving up his "fix'd place." Before he leaves, he invokes the goddess Nature to curse Goneril with sterility, or, if she must bear a child, to let it be a spiteful child who will torment her and cause her to grow old before her time. Albany, still puzzled, questions Goneril about her father, but she evades the issue, telling him not to worry.

Having heard that Goneril has just reduced his train of followers by 50, Lear re-enters, cursing his daughter for destroying his manhood. He threatens to leave and stay with Regan, convinced that she would scratch her sister's eyes out if she heard of the way in which Goneril had been treating her father. Goneril, however, quickly sends a letter to her sister, warning her that Lear is coming. Doubting the wisdom of Goneril's actions, Albany censures his wife for her decision, but she criticizes his "milky gentleness" and his "want of wisdom."

Analysis

As Kent interviews for a position as a servant in Lear's retinue, he takes on the mannerisms of the Fool. His witty humor, spoken in prose, prompts Lear to respond to him as he would to his Fool. Kent's long list of attributes that he thinks would make him a good servant, includes "to eat no fish," a Protestant virtue easily understood by an Elizabethan audience. At the opening of the scene, Kent speaks in verse but changes to prose when he takes on his disguise as a servant. Later, when he is left alone in the stocks, he will again speak in verse, assuming his true character as the noble Earl of Kent.

Oswald, addressed by Lear as "sirrah," a title for commoners, willingly carries out the wishes of his lady Goneril, linking him with the evil characters in the play. Under Goneril's instructions, he defies the King by ignoring his commands and defending himself against Lear's abusive insults. This behavior, demonstrated by a servant against a king or other noble, would have been unheard of in Shakespeare's day.

When we first meet the Fool, he offers his coxcomb to Kent, demonstrating that anyone aligning himself with the King is a fool and needs to wear the cap of the Fool. The Fool warns Kent that he cannot take "one's (Lear's) part that's out of favor" and at the same time bring himself into the good graces of those now in power, or he will soon "catch cold," or be out in the cold. Lear's Fool is often referred to by critics as a character assuming the role of the "chorus" whose function is to comment on the action of the play. The Fool speaks the bitter truth about King Lear's folly in dividing his kingdom between his two oldest daughters. He is the only character who can speak the truth without the risk of banishment. Lear, in fact, threatens to whip him if he tells a lie. To the implication that he might be calling Lear a fool, he replies, "All thy other titles thou hast given away, that thou wast born with." Kent's response, "This is not altogether fool," shows the wisdom of the Fool, who is not merely there to entertain. The Fool censures Lear for splitting his crown in the middle and giving away both parts to his daughters. "Thou bor'st thine ass on thy back o'er the dirt" alludes to one of Aesop's fables in which the miller and his son foolishly carry a donkey instead of riding on his back. The analogy is clear: both Lear and the miller have foolishly inverted the order of nature. Lear's response when the Fool asks him whether he can make use of "nothing," echoes the words first spoken regarding Cordelia.

Goneril's diatribe concerning Lear's unruly train of followers is, perhaps, not altogether unwarranted, considering the rash behavior her father has exhibited thus far in the play. Lear insists, however, that his "train are men of choice and rarest parts" and curses Goneril with sterility or at least a child who will torment her so that she too will feel the pain of a "thankless child." In spite of his protest, she reduces his train by 50 followers. Lear decides to leave immediately, certain that his daughter Regan will take him in. Confident that her sister will not "sustain him and his hundred knights," Goneril quickly sends word to her sister, informing her of Lear's arrival. Goneril's true motive for reducing Lear's train comes out by the end of the scene. She is afraid that with a hundred armed knights "He may enguard his dotage with their pow'rs, / And hold our lives in mercy." Her husband, Albany, is troubled by her actions, but she accuses him of lacking wisdom which is reminiscent of her treatment of the King.

Study Questions

1. Why does Kent speak in verse and then change to prose in the beginning of the scene?

2. Why does the Fool offer his coxcomb to Kent?

3. Why is the Fool often referred to as the chorus?

4. What behavior does Oswald demonstrate to the King?

5. Why is Goneril angry at her father in this scene?

6. In Lear's rage against his daughter Goneril, who does he think he can turn to?

7. How many of Lear's followers does Goneril take from him?

8. What does Goneril do to warn her sister of Lear's departure from Albany's palace?

9. How does the Duke of Albany feel about his wife's actions against the King?

10. What is Goneril's response to Albany's fears?

Answers

1. Kent speaks in verse because he is the Earl of Kent. He speaks in prose when he is disguised as a servant.

2. The Fool offers his coxcomb because he thinks Kent is a fool for following Lear.

3. Traditionally the chorus functions as a commentary on the action of the play. The Fool plays the role of the chorus.

4. Oswald is defiant and treats the King with disrespect.

5. Goneril tells her father that his train of followers are unruly and quarrelsome.

6. Lear says Regan will take him in.

7. Goneril reduces Lear's followers by 50.

8. Goneril writes Regan a letter warning her of Lear's arrival.

9. Albany is troubled by his wife's actions.

10. Goneril accuses Albany of a lack of wisdom in his decision-making.

Suggested Essay Topics

1. Lear's Fool is often seen as a wise character in the play. Discuss the way in which he acts as a commentator on Lear's folly. Explain why Lear tolerates his truths. Why were Kent and Cordelia banished for telling the truth? Cite examples from the play to support your view.

2. The Duke of Albany has a "milky gentleness" that annoys his wife Goneril. Explain their marriage relationship in light of the hierarchy of nature prevalent in Shakespeare's time. How does this hierarchy apply to Goneril's attitude toward her husband and father. Give examples from the play to support your answer.

Act I, Scene 5

New Characters:

Gentleman: *one of Lear's train attending to the horses*

Summary

The scene is set in the courtyard in front of Albany's palace. Preparing to leave for Regan's, Lear orders Kent to deliver a letter to her in the city of Gloucester. He urges Kent to make sure he arrives before Lear does. In an attempt to raise his master's spirits, the Fool engages in honest witty metaphors and nonsensical riddles. Lear plays the game for a short time but soon slips back into his preoccupations with his daughter's ingratitude and his fears of madness. His gentleman soon arrives with the horses, and they are on their way to Regan's.

Analysis

This short scene acts as a commentary on Lear's emotional state as he prepares himself for his new living arrangements with his middle daughter, Regan. His Fool, though annoying at times, honestly reflects his master's fears. Lear has, after all, failed, and one can imagine him contemplating his last chance. Judging by observations thus far and the opinion of the Fool on the matter, Goneril and Regan are of like mind. The Fool's honesty is no reassurance when he says, "She will taste as like this as a crab does to a crab." In his preoccupation, Lear seems unmoved by the Fool's comments as he ruminates about Cordelia. "I did her wrong" is reminiscent of the previous scene where her faults seemed small compared to Goneril's.

Lear's illusory world is no longer intact, giving him new insights concerning the worth of his daughters and new perceptions of his own identity. In the previous scene he has begun to question that identity: "Who is it that can tell me who I am?" The Fool's painful metaphor suggests that he is a snail who has given his shell, or house, away to his daughters. He considers taking Goneril's half of the kingdom back again, but the Fool interjects with "Thou shouldst

not have been old till thou hadst been wise." The intrusion of his reality leads him to invoke the heavens to "Keep me in temper, I would not be mad!" Here again, we see his belief in the natural order of things with a higher being in control of the universe.

Study Questions

1. Who is sent with a letter for Lear's daughter Regan?
2. How does the Fool expect Regan to receive her father?
3. How does Lear feel about Cordelia at this point in the play?
4. What does the Fool mean when he says that a snail has a house to put his "head in, not to give it away to his daughters"?
5. What does Lear want to do to Goneril because of her ingratitude?
6. In what way is Lear's illusory world disappearing?
7. What does the Fool mean when he says he is "old before his time?"
8. What evidence do we have that Lear believes in a higher being?
9. What is the purpose of the Fool in this scene?
10. What is the main purpose of this short scene?

Answers

1. Kent, the disguised servant of King Lear, is sent to the city of Gloucester with a letter for Regan.
2. The Fool thinks Regan will be exactly like her sister.
3. Lear feels he has not treated Cordelia properly.
4. The Fool is censuring Lear for giving his kingdom to his daughters. He feels it is an unnatural thing to do.
5. He would like to take Goneril's half of the kingdom back.
6. He has gained new insight regarding his daughter Cordelia.
7. The Fool means that Lear is "old before he is wise."

8. Lear invokes the heavens to keep him from going mad.

9. The Fool acts as an honest commentary on the King's fears.

10. This short scene reflects Lear's emotional state at this point in the play.

Suggested Essay Topics

1. Lear has lived in a world of deception and illusion thus far in the play. Discuss Lear's illusory world in relation to his three daughters. Compare these illusions to the new insights he is gaining at the end of Act I. How does he feel about his daughter Cordelia at this point in the play? Cite examples from the play to support your answer.

2. Lear has made a decision to leave his daughter Goneril's palace and live with Regan instead. How do you think he feels as he contemplates this move? Does he feel sure Regan will welcome him? Discuss his guilt abut Cordelia. Explain your answer.

Act II

Act II, Scene 1

New Character:

Curan: *a courtier at Gloucester's castle*

Summary

Curan, the courtier, informs Edmund that the Duke of Cornwall and Regan will be coming to Gloucester's castle shortly. He also gives Edmund inside information about the likelihood of war between Cornwall and Albany. Seizing the opportunity to use the Duke of Cornwall's visit to his own advantage, Edmund immediately sets his plan into action. Calling his brother Edgar from his hiding place, he warns him to flee in haste before his father can capture him. He tells Edgar that Cornwall's unexpected visit might prove dangerous to him. In an attempt to stage a convincing escape, Edmund draws his sword and urges his brother to do the same, pretending to defend himself against Edmund. He is supposedly trying to capture Edgar and bring him to his father. After Edgar's escape, Edmund, aware that Gloucester has been watching from a distance, secretly wounds himself in the arm. The sight of blood, he thinks, will impress upon his father that he has, indeed, fought a hard fight.

Gloucester approaches, demanding to know the whereabouts of Edgar. He calls for the pursuit of the villain. Edmund tells his father that Edgar tried to persuade him of "the murther of your lordship." Ironically, Edmund has supposedly warned his brother that the revenging gods are opposed to parricide, and the child is "bound to th' father." Edmund continues his deceitful tirade, declaring how "loathly opposite" he stood to Edgar's opinion and "unnatural purpose." For all this Edmund received a wound from the fleeing Edgar. Gloucester reacts with rage, calling Edgar a "murderous coward" and declaring that he will catch him and bring him "to the stake." He will use the authority of the Duke of Cornwall to bring him to justice. Edmund also accuses Edgar of calling him an "unpossessing bastard" whose word would not stand up against his if he denied writing the letter. According to Edmund's account, Edgar told him that he could, in fact, easily blame the murder plot on Edmund. More determined than ever to find Edgar, Gloucester prepares to publish his picture throughout the kingdom. Calling Edmund his "loyal and natural boy," he promises to arrange to have him acknowledged as his legal heir.

Cornwall and Regan enter, having heard the shocking news about Edgar. Quick to accept Edmund's deceitful story, Regan promptly blames Edgar's behavior on his association with Lear's "riotous knights." Having been informed by Goneril of Lear's arrival, Cornwall and Regan have decided not to stay and wait for him. Cornwall invites Edmund into his service, commending him for his virtue and obedience. Explaining why they have come, Regan asks for Gloucester's counsel concerning Goneril's "differences" with her father.

Analysis

This scene, involving the subplot, is analogous to the first scene of the play. In the main plot, King Lear is duped by his older daughters into believing they love him "more than words can wield the matter." In the subplot, Edmund deceives Gloucester about his own devotion toward his father: "by no means he could...Persuade me to the murther of your lordship." Edmund's gain is necessarily Edgar's loss. In both cases, Lear and Gloucester, through their own lack of insight, must bear the loss of one of their children. W. R. Elton sees the double plot as a "developing metaphor" in which the action in these two parts "mirror each other." (W. R. Elton,

"Double Plot in King Lear.") Gloucester's rage, triggered by the slender evidence against his son Edgar, is reminiscent of Lear's violent anger demonstrated toward Cordelia resulting in her banishment. The main plot and the subplot operate in contrapuntal fashion to render depth and a clearer perception of the play as a whole.

Curan's news about the rumored civil strife brewing between the Dukes of Albany and Cornwall is a foreshadowing of future strife in the kingdom. Edmund is an opportunist who wastes no time plotting against his brother Edgar when he hears of Albany's arrival at Gloucester's castle. He is a master at manipulating the minds of Regan and Albany and immediately gains favor in their sight.

The irony runs deep in this scene when Edmund criticizes Edgar, attributing to him the very vices that are second nature to himself. There seems to be a role reversal with Edmund being the "loyal and natural boy" instead of Edgar. The irony reaches its peak, however, when Edmund talks of warning Edgar that the gods will wreak their vengeance against parricides, and "the natural bond of child to father" must be honored. In view of Edmund's idea of nature, in which he rejects the hierarchical order in a previous scene, his fabricated story to his father is a masquerade. He is, indeed, a wolf in sheep's clothing. Gloucester's lack of insight leads him to seek the wrong villain when he asks, "Now, Edmund, where's the villain?"

Outwardly, Regan and Cornwall seem honest in administering justice in the case of Edgar. Regan, however, all too quickly links Edgar's alleged actions to her father's "riotous knights." Her decision to be gone when her father arrives at her house reveals her true character, linking her with her evil sister Goneril.

Study Questions

1. Why does Edmund ask Edgar to raise his sword against him?

2. Why is Edmund's arm bleeding in this scene?

3. What does Gloucester propose to do after Edgar's escape?

4. Who does Gloucester ask to help him find Edgar and bring him to justice?

5. Who does Regan blame for Edgar's alleged problem with his father?

6. What will the King find when he and his followers reach Regan's house?

7. Why have Cornwall and Regan come to Gloucester's castle? What do they wish to discuss with him?

8. Why does Cornwall commend Edmund?

9. Whom does Gloucester call his "loyal and natural boy"?

10. Why does Gloucester intend to publish Edgar's picture throughout the kingdom?

Answers

1. Edmund wants his father to see him attempting to prevent Edgar's escape.

2. Edmund gave himself a wound with his own sword to impress his father.

3. Gloucester says that Edgar shall not remain uncaught and proposes to send his picture throughout the kingdom.

4. Gloucester asks for the Duke of Albany's help in finding Edgar and bringing him to justice.

5. Regan blames his association with the King's "riotous knights" who, she thinks, have put him up to it.

6. The King will find that Regan and her husband are not there.

7. Cornwall and Regan have come to ask for Gloucester's advice about the quarrel between Goneril and the King.

8. Cornwall commends Edmund for his virtue and obedience.

9. Edmund is called Gloucester's "loyal and natural boy."

10. Gloucester plans to publish Edgar's picture throughout the kingdom so that someone will report having seen him, which could help matters regarding his capture.

Suggested Essay Topics

1. The subplot often functions to give depth and a clearer perception of the characters and the action in the play. Com-

pare this scene to the first scene of the play. In what way do Lear and his daughters compare to Gloucester and his sons? Discuss the analogy between Edgar and Cordelia. Cite examples from the play to support your argument.

2. Edmund's speeches in this scene are filled with irony. Discuss the irony in his account of his alleged conversation with Edgar. Why are these lines in opposition to Edgar's beliefs? Use examples from the play to support your answer.

Act II, Scenes 2 and 3

Summary

Oswald appears at Gloucester's castle, and Kent, Lear's courier, promptly recognizes him as Goneril's steward whom he had "tripp'd up by the heels" and beaten for his insolent behavior to the King only a few days before. Feigning innocence, Oswald pretends he has never seen Kent. Kent rebukes him harshly and then draws his sword, challenging Oswald to do the same. Edmund enters in response to Oswald's cries for help. Edmund's sword is drawn and Kent turns on him, but Cornwall, who has just appeared, orders them to "keep peace." Regan and Gloucester, following closely behind Cornwall, are appalled at the sight of weapons. Cornwall demands to hear an account of their differences. Continuing to rail at Oswald, Kent calls him a "cowardly rascal" whom "Nature disclaims," and who must, therefore, have been made by a tailor. Oswald defends his cowardice, telling Cornwall he has spared Kent's life because he was a "grey beard." Enraged by Oswald's outright lie and his patronizing attitude toward him, Kent rants on with irreverent expletives about this rogue "who wears no honesty."

Cornwall takes the part of Oswald, however, and calls for Kent to be put in the stocks. Kent reminds Cornwall that he serves the King, and this move will surely create ill feelings. Troubled by the effect it will have on the King, Gloucester too pleads with Cornwall to rescind his decision. Cornwall remains stoic, however, and Regan is determined to put her sister's feelings above her father's.

Left alone, Kent is optimistic about his time in the stocks. He

will catch up on some much-needed sleep and the remainder of the time he will spend whistling. Before he sleeps, he finds comfort in reading a letter from Cordelia.

Edgar's soliloquy in Scene 3 portrays him as "poor Tom," a Bedlam beggar. He will disguise himself by griming his face with filth, tying his hair in knots, and covering his nakedness with only a blanket. Fleeing from the law, he has escaped capture by hiding in the hollow of a tree.

Analysis

On the surface, it would seem that Kent's scurrilous treatment of Oswald in the beginning of the scene is excessive and unjustified. Greeting Kent with courtesy and decorum, Oswald seems undeserving of his verbal abuse. Kent immediately recognizes him as Goneril's insolent steward, however, who behaved badly to the King only a few days earlier. Kent also realizes that Oswald comes with letters against the King taking "Vanity the puppet's part." The implication is that Vanity, a character in ancient morality plays, is, in this case, personified by Goneril. Oswald repeatedly denies knowing Kent, but later he relates to Cornwall the details of his recent experience with Kent and the King. It is this pretense that Kent, who is characteristically blunt and honest, cannot tolerate. For his inability to engage in flattery, Kent is now awarded time in the stocks just as it had brought him banishment earlier. In this sense, Kent's experience is analogous to Cordelia's. Disorder flourishes in the world of the play where the honest characters are castigated and the deceitful ones rewarded.

As was true in previous scenes, lack of respect for old people is a recurring theme in the play. Cornwall refers to Kent as a "stubborn ancient knave" whom he intends to teach a lesson by putting him in the stocks. Kent's satiric retort, "Sir, I am too old to learn," lends humor to the idea that with age comes wisdom, which is in keeping with the natural order of things.

Cornwall spends much time and effort getting at the truth of the quarrel between Kent and Oswald. It is noteworthy that his abrupt decision to "Fetch forth the stocks," catching Kent and Gloucester by complete surprise, comes in the wake of Oswald's account of the King's abusiveness toward him. Cornwall's sudden decision to place Kent in the stocks is an act of defiance against the King's authority. The Duke is unmoved by Kent's appeal for the respect of his master, the King. Regan too feels it would be worse to abuse her sister's servant. To Gloucester's appeal "the King must take it ill/ That he,.../ Should have him (Kent) thus restrained," comes Cornwall's curt reply, "I'll answer that." The Duke shows no visible remorse for his act of rebellion against the King.

Left alone in the stocks, Kent speaks in verse at the end of the scene, reverting back to his true character, the noble Earl of Kent. He looks forward to perusing a letter from Cordelia, who has fortunately been informed of his disguise and his situation as servant of the King.

Scene 3 is a short account of what has happened in Edgar's life since the betrayal of his half-brother, Edmund. In his soliloquy, Edgar tells us he has been living in the hollow of a tree, escaping "the hunt." Like Kent, Edgar will also take on a disguise to preserve his life. He plans to hide in the guise of a Bedlam beggar. Bedlam is another word for Bethlehem Hospital, a London madhouse of the sixteenth century. The madmen of that day who roamed the London streets begging for food became known as "poor Toms." "Edgar I nothing am," indicates his loss of identity as Edgar, son of the Earl of Gloucester.

Study Questions

1. Why is Kent violently angry at Oswald, Goneril's steward?

2. Does Oswald pretend that Kent is a total stranger to him? What proves him wrong?

3. Why is Kent placed in the stocks?

4. What does Regan think would be worse than putting her father's servant in the stocks?

5. What is Cornwall's response to Kent's statement that he serves the King?

6. How does Gloucester feel about Kent being placed in the stocks?

7. Why does Kent speak in verse when he is alone in the stocks and in prose earlier in the scene?

8. Whose letter does Kent read before he falls asleep?

9. Where has Edgar been living since he fled from his father's castle?

10. How will he disguise himself in order to save his life?

Answers

1. Kent is angry because Oswald comes with letters against the King and pretends he has never seen Kent.

2. Oswald pretends he has never met Kent, but later he tells Cornwall the entire story.

3. Kent is placed in the stocks because Cornwall takes Oswald's side against Kent's in the quarrel.

4. Regan feels it would be worse to have her sister's steward abused than to have her father's courier put in the stocks.

5. Cornwall remains stoic about putting Kent in the stocks.

6. Gloucester feels the King will "take it ill" when he sees him in this condition.

7. When he is alone he no longer needs to maintain his disguise.

8. Kent reads a letter from Cordelia.

9. Edgar has been living in the hollow of a tree.

10. Edgar will disguise himself as Tom o' Bedlam.

Suggested Essay Topics

1. Kent has been portrayed as an honest character thus far in the play. Discuss his honesty in the light of his banishment and his time in the stocks. Compare the honest characters to the deceitful characters in the play. Is Kent's blunt honesty necessary? Cite examples from the play to support your answer.

2. Kent and Edgar both assume disguises in the play. Compare and contrast their reasons for the disguise. Discuss the dif-

ferences in their physical disguises. How are their disguises
alike? Is Edgar in greater danger than Kent? Explain your
answer.

Act II, Scene 4

Summary

Lear, his Fool, and his Gentleman arrive at Gloucester's castle.
The King finds it puzzling that Cornwall and Regan have left their
house on the night of his expected arrival without sending a message to explain. Kent who is still in the stocks, greets his master.
Shocked to see his courier in this shameful condition, the King
thinks it must be a joke. Kent tells Lear it was Regan and Cornwall
who placed him there. In disbelief, Lear argues with Kent, bandy-
ing back and forth until the King finally faces the truth. He insists
that they would not dare engage in such an act of disrespect toward the King through his messenger. Incensed by Cornwall and
Regan's actions, Lear calls it a "violent outrage" that is "worse than
murther." When asked for a reason by the King, Kent truthfully
admits that he demonstrated "more man than wit," when he drew
his sword on Oswald.

Commenting on the action, the Fool recites fanciful rhymes
about Lear's problems with his daughters, observing that poor fathers "make their children blind" while rich fathers "see their children kind." Asking for his daughter's whereabouts, Lear is told she
is within. Determined to rectify the situation with Kent, Lear presently enters the castle, asking the others to stay behind. Kent inquires about the King's decreased train of followers. The Fool tells
him that it is a question deserving time in the stocks. When Kent
asks why, the Fool answers in prose and verse alluding to the stormy
times ahead.

Lear and Gloucester enter with the news that Cornwall and
Regan refuse to speak to Lear, giving the excuse that they are sick
and weary from traveling all night. Lear requests a better answer
from Gloucester, who discreetly reminds the King that the "fiery
quality" of the Duke is at the heart of the problem. Lear's explosive
reply calls for vengeance and death. He demands to speak with

the Duke of Cornwall and Regan immediately, but Gloucester simply states that he has already informed them. The King's fury increases as he excoriates the "fiery Duke." His mood suddenly changes, however, when he considers that the Duke may not be well. When he is reminded of Kent's humiliation in the stocks, however, he is sure this act is a symbol of the death of his royal power as king. He again calls for the Duke and Regan to "come forth and hear me."

Gloucester enters with Cornwall and Regan. They both greet him with proper decorum, addressing him as "your Grace" and telling him they are glad to see him. Kent is set free. The King promptly begins his diatribe complaining about Goneril's depravity and her "Sharp-toothed unkindness," but Regan steps in to defend her sister. She asks him to return to Goneril and apologize for having "wrong'd her." Lear falls on his knees begging Regan to take him in. Annoyed, Regan tells him to stop his unsightly tricks and go back to Goneril's house. Cursing Goneril and swearing never to live with her again, he promises Regan that she will never have his curse.

The King asks Regan who put his man in the stocks, but is interrupted by Oswald's arrival. Recognizing him as Goneril's steward, Lear orders him out of his sight and again demands to know who stocked his servant. This time he is interrupted by Goneril's arrival. Seeing her, the King invokes the heavens to come down and take his part. Lear admonishes her for daring to face him, but she feigns innocence and justifies her past behavior. Cornwall finally admits having put Lear's man in the stocks.

Regan approaches Lear, trying to persuade him to return to her sister's for the remainder of the month, dismiss half his train, and then return to her after she has had time to make provisions for his arrival. Infuriated, Lear declares that he would rather "abjure all roofs" than give up 50 of his men. Goneril casually tells him it is his choice. Rebuffing her with contempt, he reminds her he can stay with Regan and keep his 100 knights. Regan's quick reply, "Not altogether so," is a reminder that she has not yet made preparations for him and his large train of followers. What's more, she decides to reduce his train further and allow him only 25 followers. Lear's painful outcry "I gave you all" is met with a cold response from Regan. After some thought, he decides to go with Goneril where he will at least be allowed 50 knights, but Goneril and Regan proceed to cut his entire train and only allow him the use of their own servants. Condemning his daughters as "unnatural hags," Lear swears he will go mad rather than succumb to weeping. In "high rage" the King wanders out into the impending storm while Goneril and Regan affirm their resolution to cut off the services of all his knights. Regan and Cornwall then implore Gloucester to "Shut up your doors" against the wild night and leave Lear to his own devices.

Analysis

Lear's Fool places himself in the middle of the action in this scene with a variety of poignant phrases that again expose the truth of Lear's folly in relation to his daughters.

> Fathers that wear rags
> Do make their children blind,
> But fathers that bear bags
> Shall see their children kind.

With his use of metaphor, the Fool satirizes Lear's foolishness in giving away his "bags" of money to his daughters. In only a matter of weeks, Goneril and Regan have changed from overt expressions of love and kindness before his division of the kingdom to a dogged blindness to their father's needs after they inherit all his money. When Kent is placed in the stocks by Cornwall and Regan, the Fool's comment, "Winter's not gone yet," bears the implication that the worst is not over. The Fool clearly recognizes the act of irreverence and rebellion to the King inherent in their actions toward Kent, his messenger.

In the opening part of the scene, the Fool thinks Kent has been remiss in delivering an answer to Lear's letter from Regan. According to the Fool, Kent, therefore, wears "cruel garters" made of wood because he has been "overlusty at legs," or, run from his duty instead of tending to the service of the King.

The Fool foreshadows the imminent storm at the end of this scene when he talks in rhyme about those who "serve and seek for gain." They will, the Fool says, "pack when it begins to rain,/ And leave thee in the storm." The image is clear, working on the literal

as well as the symbolic level of the play. Lear is, indeed, left out in
the storm as Regan counsels Gloucester to "Shut up your doors."

The Fool's advice to "set thee to school to an ant, to teach thee
there's no laboring i' th' winter" alludes to the Bible and would have
been readily understood by audiences of Shakespeare's day.

> Go to the ant, thou sluggard;
> consider her ways and be wise:
> Which having no guide, overseer, or ruler,
> Provideth her meat in the summer,
> and gathereth her food in the harvest.
>
> Proverbs 6: 6-8

Even the ant is wise enough to know there is no labor in the
winter. Lear, in the winter of his life, is likened to a great wheel going
downhill and finally deserted. But in the prophetic words of the
Fool himself, "the Fool will tarry, the Fool will stay."

Lear's characteristic tendency to judge his daughters' love on
a mathematical scale is readily apparent in this scene. In the first
scene he promises to extend the "largest bounty" to the one who
"loves us most." In the same mode, he refuses to live with Goneril
after she dismisses 50 of his men. On the other hand, when Regan
refuses to take him in unless he reduces his train of followers to 25,
Lear suddenly decides to live with Goneril whose "fifty yet doth
double five and twenty,/ And thou art twice her love." Ultimately,
of course, both daughters decide they will receive the King "But
not one follower." Devastated, Lear stumbles out into the storm in
"high rage."

By admonishing Lear to apologize to Goneril, Regan commits
an atrocity well recognized in Elizabethan England. The King would
not, by the laws of society, ask the forgiveness of his daughter, nor
would he be forced to beg, though ironically, for food and raiment.
Lear invokes the gods to touch him with "noble anger." He vows to
avenge his daughters who are "unnatural hags." Some critics feel
his behavior at this point in the play becomes almost childish.
Hovering at the verge of a temper tantrum, he fights back "women's
weapons, water-drops." The alliteration and rhythm forces a heavy
emphasis on each word, creating a tone that demonstrates Lear's
disdain for acting "womanish," and, thereby, destroying the natu-

ral order.

Study Questions

1. Why is the King puzzled when he arrives at Gloucester's castle?

2. Whom does the King see in the stocks? Why was he put in the stocks?

3. Which metaphor does the Fool use to foreshadow the storm?

4. What excuse do Cornwall and Regan give for not greeting the King when he arrives at Gloucester's castle?

5. Why has Lear come to Regan's house?

6. Why does Lear fall on his knees to Regan?

7. How many of Lear's men has Goneril dismissed when he arrives at Gloucester's castle?

8. How many men does Regan want him to have in his train?

9. Whom does Lear refer to as "unnatural hags"?

10. Where does Lear go after his daughters reduce his train of followers to nothing?

Answers

1. The King cannot understand the reason for Cornwall and Regan's absence on the night of his expected arrival.

2. The King sees Kent, his messenger, in the stocks. He has been placed there by Cornwall.

3. The Fool says that those who serve for gain "Will pack when it begins to rain,/ And leave thee in the storm."

4. Cornwall and Regan say they are tired and sick from traveling all night.

5. Lear and Goneril have quarreled, and he wants Regan to take him to live with her.

6. On his knees, Lear begs Regan to take him in.

7. Goneril has reduced Lear's train of followers by 50 men.

8. Regan thinks 25 in his train would be an ample amount.

9. Lear refers to his oldest two daughters as "unnatural hags."

10. Lear goes out into the storm and braves the "wild night."

Suggested Essay Topics

1. The Fool's purpose in the play is to comment on the action. Discuss the poem that begins "Fathers that wear rags." Explain the metaphors in this poem. How do they apply to Lear and his daughters? Cite examples from the play to support your answer.

2. Lear's daughters have usurped his power by depriving him of his entire train of followers by the end of the scene. Compare and contrast the characters of Goneril and Regan in this scene. How are they alike? How are they different? Why does the King call them "unnatural hags? Give examples from the play to support your answer.

Act III

Act III, Scene 1

Summary

On the heath near Gloucester's castle, Kent, braving the storm, immediately recognizes the King's Gentleman. He informs Kent that the King is "contending with the fretfrul elements" with only his Fool to keep him company. The Gentleman reports that Lear roams bareheaded on the stormy heath, striving to "outscorn...the wind and rain," as his loyal Fool desperately tries to comfort him.

Kent quickly realizes the Gentleman is one whom he can trust. He discloses to him rumors of a division between Albany and Cornwall, though it is still not out in the open. The King of France, Cordelia's husband, has sent his spies to attend the households of Cornwall and Albany as servants. Under their surveillance, quarrels and plots between the two houses have been reported and news of their abusiveness to the King has reached France. Kent thinks "something deeper" also may be brewing. France's secret invasion of England's "scattered" kingdom is imminent. Kent asks the Gentleman to go to Dover to disclose to its citizens the "unnatural" treatment of the King. Assuring the Gentleman of his noble birth, Kent gives him a ring to hand to Cordelia whom he will most likely find in Dover. He explains that she will confirm Kent's true identity. The two then part ways, searching for Lear in the storm and agreeing to give the signal when he is found.

Analysis

This scene functions to inform us of Lear's struggle against the elements on the stormy heath. The loyalty of the Fool who accompanies Lear is reminiscent of the previous scene where the Fool confirms his constancy and allegiance. When others "leave thee in the storm," he says, "I will tarry, the Fool will stay." Attempting to ease the King's sorrows, the Fool "labors to outjest/ His heart-strook injuries." If the fool's candid jesting about Lear's lack of good judgment as a father and a king has been annoying at times, one can only stand in awe of his loving care and devotion to the King in the worst of all possible situations, the storm on the heath.

In this scene we hear further rumors of the possibility of a war between the Dukes of Cornwall and Albany. Curan, a courtier in Gloucester's castle, has already predicted the conflict in his conversation with Edmund in Act II, Scene 1. It should be noted, however, that the dissension between the two households is likely to be led by Goneril rather than Albany.

In Cordelia's letter, read by Kent while he was in the stocks in Act II, Scene 2, she writes that she has been "inform'd/ Of my (Kent's) obscured course." In this scene, we learn that Cordelia's informers are, indeed, spies acting as servants in the houses of Cornwall and Albany. Kent informs the Gentleman that Cordelia will most likely be in Dover. Together with the French Army, she waits there to rectify her sisters' abuses toward her father, the King. In this scene, we are given a glimmer of hope that Cordelia will liberate her father from the hands of her self-seeking sisters. Certain that the recent events leading to the King's condition will anger his loyal citizens in Dover, Kent sends the Gentleman to spread the news.

Study Questions

1. Where is the King at this point in the play?

2. Who has stayed with the King to give him comfort?

3. What are the rumors concerning Cornwall and Albany?

4. Who are the spies sent to England by the King of France?

5. What news do France's spies bring regarding King Lear?

6. Where does Kent think Cordelia will be staying?

7. What does Kent tell the Gentleman to show Cordelia as proof of Kent's identity?

8. Before the Gentleman goes to Dover, what does he do?

9. What does the French Army intend to do in England?

10. What is Cordelia's purpose for her temporary stay in Dover?

Answers

1. Lear's Gentleman tells Kent that the King is in the storm on the heath outside of Gloucester's castle.

2. Only the Fool accompanies the King on the heath.

3. It is rumored that there is division between Cornwall and Albany, leading to civil strife in the kingdom.

4. The spies act as servants in the households of Cornwall and Albany.

5. The spies bring the news that King Lear has had to bear the abuses of Goneril and Regan, his daughters.

6. Kent thinks Cordelia is waiting in Dover.

7. Kent instructs the Gentleman to give Cordelia a ring as proof of Kent's identity.

8. The Gentleman helps to find Lear in the storm.

9. The French Army intends to stage a secret attack on England.

10. Cordelia waits, along with the French Army, to rectify her sisters' injustices to the King.

Suggested Essay Topics

1. The Fool has been censuring his master for his lack of judgment as a king but stays with him and helps alleviate his suffering in the storm on the heath. Write an essay discussing the Fool's loyalty to the King in the storm. Why is he critical of the King? Why does he stay with him when others desert him? Cite examples from the play to prove your point.

2. Cordelia seems to be associated with Kent thus far in the play. Both have been banished, but she has stayed in touch with Kent. Compare and contrast the characters of Cordelia and Kent. How do they personify the good or evil inherent in the play? Explain your answer using examples from the play.

Act III, Scene 2

Summary

The groundwork has already been laid by the Gentleman in the previous scene informing us of Lear's struggle against the fierce storm on the heath. As the scene opens, Lear fervently calls upon the winds to blow, the lightning to "Spit, fire," the rain to "drench the steeples," and the thunder to crack open "nature's moulds" and spill the seeds that make "ingrateful man." The Fool counsels Lear to submit to his daughters' authority over him and beg to be taken out of the storm. He reasons that it would be better to "court holy-water," or, in other words, flatter his daughters, than to continue braving the stormy night. Ignoring the Fool's pleas, he addresses the elements, telling them he will show them no unkindness since he never gave them his kingdom, and, therefore, they owe him nothing. His mood quickly swings, however, as he rails against the rain, wind, thunder, and lightning, suspecting that they are, after all, only the "servile ministers" of his "pernicious daughters" fighting a battle against him.

The Fool, continuing his jesting in rhyme, again censures the King, telling him that the person who has "a house to put 's head in" has a good brain. In a strained attempt to control his passions, Lear swears he will be the epitome of patience.

Kent enters with expressions of terror at the night sky that is unparalleled in his memory. Lear calls on the gods to wreak their stormy vengeance on criminals who have never been brought to justice. He considers himself above them, stating that he is "More sinn'd against than sinning." Kent gently guides the "bare-headed" Lear into a hovel that provides shelter from the storm. He talks of turning back to Gloucester's castle with the intention of forcing them to receive him.

Lear tells the Fool his wits are beginning to turn. For the first time he shows compassion for him, asking him whether he is cold. The Fool delays the end of the scene, quoting a long prophecy in rhymed verse.

Analysis

In the sixteenth century, the theaters were relatively devoid of stage props. Shakespeare's setting of the storm on the heath is, therefore, largely dependent upon the strong and vigorous imagery of Lear's language. Though the Fool disagrees, preferring a "dry house" to the stormy night, Lear calls upon the elements to wreak their vengeance on "ingrateful man." With metaphors, he paints an image of rain, wind, thunder, and lightning that provide the setting for the storm.

> Blow, winds, and crack your cheeks! rage, blow!
> You cataracts and hurricanoes, spout
> Till you have drench'd our steeples, (drown'd) the cocks!
> You sulph'rous and thought-executing fires,
> Vaunt-couriers of oak-cleaving thunderbolts,
> Singe my white head!

Personifying the elements, Lear sees them as "servile ministers" to his daughters who are engaging them in a battle to destroy him. Hence, the storm outside becomes analogous to Lear's inner struggle in his chaotic world where the political forces, who are now his daughters, threaten to destroy him. Having lost his powers when he gave away his kingdom, he is as vulnerable to his daughters' vengeance as he is to the all-encompassing storm when he roams bare-headed on the wild and barren heath.

Lear calls on the all-shaking thunder to "[c]rack nature's moulds" and spill the seeds that create "ingrateful man." J. F. Danby notes that the thunder acts as the King's agent that carries out the "King's desires in annihilating the corrupted world of man" (*Shakespeare's Doctrine of Nature*, p. 183). Lear, however, cannot, at this point in the drama, identify with that corruption. He still feels he is "More sinn'd against than sinning."

In ancient times people were in constant fear that they would, by some inadvertent act, anger the gods who would, in turn, threaten to destroy them. Though *King Lear* is set in pre-Christian times, Shakespeare's audience would have held similar views. The audience harbored a strong belief in the natural hierarchy of things, which creates a perfect harmony among all stages of being all the way down to inanimate objects. This intricate balance could be upset, however. If, for example, a king was dethroned, as is true in the case of King Lear, God might show his wrath through frightening storms. Shakespeare's *Julius Caesar* is comparable in that the storm is conjured up by the gods to avenge the impending assassination of Caesar. Casca trembles at the "scolding winds" attributing the storm to a world that has become "too saucy with the gods," incensing "them to send destruction" (*Julius Caesar,* Act I, Scene 3). Kent's misgivings about the storm are analogous to Casca's when Kent says that he has never seen "such sheets of fire, such bursts of horrid thunder" since he was a man. Casca echoes Kent's feelings when he makes claims to have seen unsettling storms in the past "But never till to-night, never till now,/ Did I go through a tempest dropping fire" (*Julius Caesar,* Act I, Scene 3).

Lear's indulgence in self-pity is all-pervading in this scene until the tone shifts suddenly with "My wits begin to turn." In a sudden flow of compassion, Lear remembers the humanity of his Fool, and, in fact, his own. "Come on, my boy. How dost, my boy? Art cold?/ I am cold myself." Lear's search for straw in order to warm himself humbles him as he realizes that necessity makes all human conditions relative.

The Fool's last speech delays his exit with a prophecy that seems to confuse time and place. His repeated use of the word "when" is anticipatory, though our immediate reaction to the first few lines is that these circumstances are not reserved for the future, but do, in fact, already reflect the evil world of the play. Reaching no conclusion, the Fool tells us that he is simply predicting the prophecy of Merlin who has not yet been born. The audience realizes then that it has attempted to follow his nonsensical rhyme to no avail.

Study Questions

1. How does Lear set the scene at the beginning?

2. How does Lear compare his daughters to the elements?

3. What does the Fool beg Lear to do to get out of the storm?

4. Who later joins Lear and the Fool in the storm?

5. Where does Kent finally lead Lear to shelter him from the storm?

6. What does Kent plan to do after he finds shelter for Lear and the Fool?

7. How does Lear express his compassion for his Fool?

8. What does Lear wear on his head when he goes out into the storm?

9. Whose prophecy does the Fool recite?

10. According to the King, who has sent the terrible storm on the heath?

Answers

1. Lear uses imagery depicting the storm on the heath.

2. Lear personifies the elements as "servile ministers" of his daughters who are trying to destroy him.

3. The Fool begs Lear to ask his daughters' blessing so they will take him in.

4. Kent joins Lear and the Fool in the storm.

5. Kent leads Lear into a hovel to shelter him from the wind and the rain.

6. Kent plans to go back to Gloucester's castle to see whether he will receive him.

7. Lear feels sorry for the Fool, inviting him into his hovel and asking him whether he is cold.

8. Lear goes into the storm bare-headed.

9. The Fool recites the prophecy of Merlin who has not yet been born.

10. Lear thinks the gods have sent the storm to punish the secret crimes that have never been brought to justice.

Suggested Essay Topics

1. In Shakespeare's day, there were relatively few stage props in the theater. Discuss the way in which Shakespeare sets the scene through the character of King Lear. Discuss Lear's use of metaphorical language to depict the storm. Relate the outer storm to Lear's inner turmoil in this scene. Give examples to support your answer.

2. The storm on the heath is viewed by Lear as a punishment to the people for their wrongdoings. Write an essay analyzing the idea that storms were a punishment by God. Discuss the storm in relation to the loss of King Lear's power and the resulting chaos after he divided his kingdom between his two daughters. Cite illustrations from the play to support your view.

Act III, Scene 3

Summary

Taking Edmund into his confidence, Gloucester informs him that Cornwall and Regan have taken over the use of his castle, castigating him for attempting to help the King. They have forbidden Gloucester to seek any aid for the King and adamantly prohibit him to talk about him.

Edmund responds as his father expects him to, expressing surprise at such actions which are most "savage and unnatural." Gloucester tells Edmund there is division between the Duke of Cornwall and the Duke of Albany. He asks Edmund not to divulge the dangerous contents of a letter he has received containing the news of a power ready to avenge the injuries done to the King. The letter is presently in Gloucester's closet under lock and key.

Instructing Edmund to cover for him at the castle in case Cornwall asks, Gloucester resolves to find the King and help relieve his misery. He tells Edmund that he has been threatened with death for taking the King's part and warns him to be careful.

Left alone, Edmund immediately decides to inform the Duke of Cornwall of all that his father has told him, including the contents of the letter. With his eye on his father's title as Duke of

Gloucester, Edmund intends to expose him to Cornwall and, thereby, gain advantage over his own father.

Analysis

This short scene functions as an interim to the actions of Kent, Lear, and the Fool on the heath. It allows the trio enough time to reach the hovel in the next scene and keeps the audience abreast of the most recent developments in the subplot.

If there has been any doubt thus far in the play, this scene reveals Edmund's complete depravity. His cunning deception and betrayal of his father establishes him as an evil character in the play. Adept at covering his guilt, Edmund reacts appropriately to Gloucester's account of Cornwall and Regan's treatment of the King which is "Most savage and unnatural." But the minute Gloucester's back is turned, he decides to expose his father to Cornwall. Edmund is an opportunist and will stop at nothing, even the threat of death to his father, to gain power.

Gloucester has been caught in a precarious situation between his loyalty to his former master, the King, and his fear of offending Cornwall and Regan. In this scene, he finally takes a stand against the injuries imposed upon the King. It is not until Cornwall and Regan's harsh takeover of his castle, however, along with their directive to break all communication with the King, that he vows to side with Lear. The contents of the letter seemingly offer hope for some respite from the King's desperate situation. With the letter locked safely in his closet, Gloucester finally makes his death-defying decision to leave his castle and "incline to the King." We will later learn that the power that is "already footed" is that of the King of France and Cordelia, who are waiting on the shore near Dover with an army. For the first time since the division of the kingdom, there is hope that the tide will turn, restoring Lear's kingdom back to its natural order.

Study Questions

1. Why do Cornwall and Regan refuse to grant Gloucester the use of his own castle?

2. How does Edmund feel about the abusive treatment of the King?

3. What news does Gloucester's dangerous letter contain?

4. What powers are "already footed" in this scene according to Gloucester?

5. Where does Gloucester keep the letter?

6. What does Edmund decide to do about the news his father has given him?

7. Why does Edmund betray his father's trust in him?

8. What does Gloucester tell Edmund to say to Cornwall if he asks for him?

9. What will be the penalty if Cornwall discovers Gloucester's intentions?

10. In what way does this scene function as an interim scene?

Answers

1. Cornwall and Regan are punishing Gloucester for giving help to the King.

2. Edmund claims it is "savage and unnatural," but he feels otherwise.

3. We may assume that the letter talks of powers that are waiting to avenge the abusive treatment of the King.

4. The King of France and Cordelia, we will learn later, are waiting on the shore near Dover with an army.

5. Gloucester has locked the letter in the closet.

6. When Gloucester leaves, Edmund immediately decides to impart the information to Cornwall.

7. Edmund wants his father's title as Earl of Gloucester.

8. Gloucester asks Edmund to tell Cornwall he is sick in bed.

9. Gloucester has been threatened with death for associating with the King and offering him help in his time of need.

10. This scene functions as an interim scene, breaking the action of Lear, Kent, and the Fool on the heath.

Suggested Essay Topics

1. Edmund is seen as a depraved character throughout the play. Write an essay comparing his behavior in this scene to his first speech in Act I, Scene 2. What were his aspirations in this soliloquy? Is he beginning to fulfill his desires in life by Act III, Scene 3? Cite examples from the play to support your view.

2. Gloucester's actions are commendable in this scene. Discuss Gloucester's courage in defying Cornwall and Regan. Why is he courageous? What are his motives? Is he a loyal subject of the King? Explain your answer.

Act III, Scene 4

Summary

Seeking shelter from the raging storm on the heath, Kent repeatedly prods Lear to enter the hovel. At first he rebuffs Kent, asking him to leave him alone, but the King finally replies that the storm invading his body is scarcely felt since the tempest in his mind is a "greater malady." Ranting on about "filial ingratitude," he reproachfully alludes to his daughters who, he thinks, "tear this hand" that feeds them. Vowing to refrain from weeping, he firmly resolves to endure, though his daughters have shut him out on a night like this. Calling their names through the din of the storm, he reminds them that he "gave all." He promptly checks himself, afraid he will go mad. He decides to shun that kind of talk. Kent responds positively and again urges him to enter the hovel. Lear finally agrees to go in, but asks Kent and his Fool to enter first. He promises to follow them after he has said a prayer. Praying with heartfelt compassion for the poor homeless and unfed wretches, he is remorseful for having taken "too little care of this."

As Lear ends his prayer, a strange voice is heard. Rushing out of the hovel, the Fool cautions Lear not to enter since there is a spirit inhabiting the shelter. Responding to Kent's command, Edgar, disguised as Tom o' Bedlam, appears from the hovel, muttering incoherent phrases about the "foul fiend" who is following him. Lear immediately perceives him as one who has been swindled by

Goneril and Regan, but Kent informs Lear that this man has no daughters. Lear is not convinced. He is sure that nothing but "Those pelican daughters" could have brought the madman to this pass.

The disguised Edgar portrays himself as a former servingman who has lived a life of questionable morals. The King contrasts Edgar to the three sophisticates: Lear, Kent, and the Fool. He recognizes Edgar as "the thing itself," devoid of all the trappings that distinguish man from a "bare, fork'd animal." Identifying with Tom's madness, Lear tears at his own clothes that are only "lendings" from nature.

Gloucester enters with a torch. The disguised Edgar identifies him as the "foul (fiend) Flibbertigibbet" who roams the streets at night. Gloucester gives an account of the impossible situation with Lear's daughters, explaining their command to bar the doors of his castle, shutting Lear out in the storm. He assures the King that he has come to take him to an outbuilding near his castle where he will be given food to eat. Lear, in his madness, responds by requesting a word with the philosopher, Tom o' Bedlam. In his concern for the King whose "wits begin t' unsettle," Kent implores Gloucester to extend the offer of food and shelter once more.

Gloucester empathizes with the mad Lear whose "daughters seek his death." He tells the disguised Kent that he had a son who also sought his life, and it has "craz'd my wits." Ironically, he makes a positive reference to the banished Kent who had predicted this would happen. Gloucester finally convinces the King to take shelter in the hovel, but Lear will only go in if his philosopher, Tom o' Bedlam, will keep him company. Humoring the King, Kent and Gloucester usher all of them into the shelter. Tom o' Bedlam echoes a familiar English ballad as the scene closes.

Analysis

The storm on the heath is symbolic of the tempest in Lear's mind. He censures Kent for his excessive concern over bodily comforts as he repeatedly urges Lear to go into the hovel. "Thou think'st 'tis much that this contentious storm/ Invades us to the skin; so 'tis to thee." On the edge of madness, Lear is tormented by a "greater malady" bringing visions of his unkind daughters shutting him out on such a night. The storm outside is scarcely felt when it is met by a stronger affliction which is that of "Filial Ingratitude." Agonizing over his misfortunes, the tortured Lear can only see others' adversities in terms of his own. As he encounters Edgar, disguised as Tom o' Bedlam, in the hovel, he repeatedly insists that it was Tom's daughters who brought him to this state of madness. "Didst thou give all to thy daughters? And/ art thou come to this?" When Kent interjects, "He hath no daughters, sir," Lear threatens him with death, calling him a traitor for opposing his king.

The storm on the heath symbolizes not only Lear's emotional turmoil, but also the disorderly tumult pervading the entire kingdom. There are rumors of wars between the Dukes of Cornwall and Albany, and Edmund intends to join forces with them. Deceit runs rampant as children turn against their parents, and the honest characters, Kent and Edgar, must disguise themselves for their very survival.

Lear's self-centered obsession with his own difficulties, however, begins to turn as he prays for the "Poor naked wretches" out in the pitiless storm. Reflecting on the plight of the homeless and hungry left without shelter in the storm, he chides himself for having taken "Too little care of this!" L. C. Knights has observed that, "This is pity, not self-pity; and condemnation of others momentarily gives way to self-condemnation." (*Shakespearean Themes*, p. 104) It is only momentary, however, and Lear again indulges in self-pity as he lashes out at his "pelican daughters."

Disguised as Tom o' Bedlam, Edgar's description of himself as a former servingman portrays the vision of a man who embodies all worldly vices: "False of heart, light of ear, bloody of hand; hog in sloth, fox in stealth, wolf in greediness, dog in madness, lion in prey." He has, in fact, descended from a human being to a "poor, bare, fork'd animal."

Lear's vision of Tom o' Bedlam as "the thing itself" stands in sharp contrast to the sophisticated three. Stripped of his power and rejected by his daughters, Lear lapses into a sudden visionary madness in which he longs for the natural state "unaccommodated man." In his incongruous endeavor to escape his true identity as a dignified king, he tears at his clothes, muttering "Off, off, you lendings." Edgar later becomes Lear's philosopher, whom he takes to a hovel as a companion. It is noteworthy that Lear, who usually speaks in verse, reverts to prose in this speech as he descends from sophisticated humanity into madness.

The main plot and the subplot are analogous in the scene when the feigned madness of Edgar is held in juxtaposition to the actual madness of Lear. Gloucester's heartbreak concerning his son, who allegedly sought his life, echoes Lear's devastating situation with his daughters who also seek his death. Confiding in Kent about his own griefs, Gloucester compares them to the King's: "Thou sayest the King grows mad, I'll tell thee, friend,/ I am almost mad my-self." Ironically, he talks of "good Kent," unaware it is, indeed, the loyal Kent whom he is addressing. It is a strange paradox that Kent must hide his true identity from the King, just as Edgar must disguise himself from his father, Gloucester. In both the main plot and the subplot, the "good" characters must disguise themselves while the evil ones parade about openly.

Study Questions

1. What does the storm on the heath symbolize?
2. Who is Edgar in disguise?
3. What type of clothing does Tom o' Bedlam wear?
4. According to Lear, who are the three sophisticated ones?
5. Who does Lear say is the "thing itself"?
6. Whom does Lear pity in his prayer on the heath?
7. What is Gloucester carrying as he enters the hovel?
8. What does Edgar call Gloucester when he approaches the hovel?
9. How does Gloucester's situation compare to Lear's?
10. Why has Gloucester come out into the storm?

Answers

1. The storm symbolizes the tempest in Lear's mind.
2. Edgar is disguised as Tom o' Bedlam, a madman.
3. Tom o' Bedlam wears only a blanket.

4. The three sophisticated persons are Lear, Kent, and the Fool.

5. Edgar in disguise is referred to as the "thing itself." He is natural, unaccommodated man.

6. Lear pities the homeless and hungry who have no place to go for shelter from the storm.

7. Gloucester is carrying a torch into the hovel.

8. Edgar calls him the foul fiend who walks the streets at night.

9. Gloucester and Lear both have children who seek their death.

10. Gloucester has come to find Lear and offer him food and shelter in an outbuilding near the castle.

Suggested Essay Topics

1. Lear's prayer is a turning point from self-pity to compassion for the "houseless heads" and "unfed sides" who are left to fend for themselves in the storm. Write an essay comparing and contrasting Lear's prayer with his speeches in the rest of the scene. Does he show compassion to others in this scene? If so, in what way? Cite examples from the play to support your view.

2. Lear sees Edgar, disguised as Tom o' Bedlam, representing "the thing itself; unaccommodated man." Write an essay explaining the meaning of these words in relation to the rest of the scene. Why does Lear wish to become like Edgar? Why does he tear off his clothes? Give examples from the play to defend your answer.

Act III, Scene 5

Summary

Acting as an informant against his father, Edmund convinces Cornwall that Gloucester is guilty of treason. Determined to have his revenge, Cornwall now reasons that Edgar's plot to kill his father was not entirely due to his brother's "evil disposition" but was, in fact, provoked by Gloucester himself. Bellying his evil motive, Edmund produces Gloucester's supposed letter as evidence that he has been supplying secret information to France. Edmund invokes the heavens to witness his regret that he should have detected his own father's treason. Cornwall rewards Edmund with his new title as Earl of Gloucester and urges him to find his father so that he can be apprehended. In an "aside" to the audience, Edmund voices his wish that he might find Gloucester "comforting the King," which would augment Cornwall's suspicions. He then turns to Cornwall, assuring him of his loyalty to the kingdom in spite of the conflict it will cause between him and his father. Confident that he can trust Edmund, Cornwall assures him that he will love him as his own son (better than Edmund's own father).

Analysis

We again see the development of the subplot in this scene in which Edmund uses Gloucester's letter as evidence of his guilt. Unlike Edgar's, Edmund's disguise is spiritual, rather than physical, as he hides behind an innocent façade, hoping to gain undeserved power and wealth at others' expense. Cloaking his deception in glossy language, Edmund laments the fact that he must "repent to be just." The irony is clear as Cornwall puts his complete trust in Edmund, promising to help him bear the loss of his father by offering himself as "a (dearer) father."

Cornwall is obviously being gulled by Edmund which becomes even more apparent in his "aside" to the audience. In his depravity, Edmund guilefully demonstrates his disloyalty to both Cornwall and Gloucester. "If I find him comforting the King, it will stuff his suspicion more fully." Turning to Cornwall, he vows to persevere in his "course of loyalty," but he is, in fact, only loyal to his own ambition of becoming the Duke of Gloucester.

Edmund calls upon the heavens to look with pity on his adversity: "O heavens! that this treason were not; or not I the detector!" He is fully aware that his piety will impress Cornwall. We are, however, reminded of Edmund's renunciation of the supernatural in Act I, Scene 2 when he condemns those who are "sick in fortune" for blaming their plight on the heavens. Unknown to Cornwall, Edmund is only calling on the god of the natural world in view of his lack of belief in the supernatural.

Filled with a desire for revenge against Gloucester for taking the King's part against him, Cornwall, no less than Edgar, carries on an illusion of fairness and integrity throughout the scene. Reaching the height of all absurdity, he vows to replace Gloucester as a loving father to Edmund.

Study Questions

1. What does Edmund produce as evidence of Gloucester's treason?

2. What important information does the letter contain?

3. How does Cornwall reward Edmund for being his informant against Gloucester?

4. Why does Edmund call upon the heavens?

5. What will Cornwall do to Gloucester for his crime of treason?

6. What is Edmund's main ambition?

7. What does Cornwall think might have been the cause of Edgar's plot to murder his father?

8. What does Cornwall promise to do to replace the loss of Edmund's father?

9. What is Cornwall's attitude as a Duke in this scene?

10. How will Cornwall search for the Duke of Gloucester?

Answers

1. Edmund shows Cornwall the supposed letter that Gloucester received from France.

2. The letter, it can be assumed, contains news of France's impending invasion of England.

3. Cornwall rewards Edmund by giving him the new title of the Duke of Gloucester.

4. Edmund calls upon the heavens to pity him in his adversity.

5. Cornwall will apprehend Gloucester when he is found.

6.   Edmund hopes to replace his father as Earl of Gloucester.

7.   Cornwall thinks that Gloucester might have provoked Edgar to plot the death of his father.

8.   Cornwall promises Edmund that he will love him even "dearer" than his own father would.

9.   Cornwall pretends to possess the qualities of fairness and integrity and will see that justice is done.

10. Cornwall asks Edmund to bring his father back to him.

Suggested Essay Topics

1.   Edmund is the epitome of deception, manipulating Cornwall for his own advantage. Write an essay demonstrating the irony of his relationship with Cornwall in this scene. How does Edmund deceive the Duke? Why is this deception ironic? What does Cornwall gain from his contact with Edmund? Cite examples from the drama to support your point.

2.   Cornwall plans to avenge Gloucester for supplying secret information to the King of France. Discuss Gloucester's threat to Cornwall. Why has Cornwall forbade him to see King Lear? How would Gloucester's loyalty to Lear affect the new divided kingdom? Explain your answer.

Act III, Scene 6

Summary

In an outbuilding near his castle, Gloucester shelters Lear from the raging storm on the heath. Kent thanks Gloucester for his kindness, afraid that the King's "wits have given way to impatience." Promising his quick return, Gloucester leaves Kent, Edgar, and the Fool with Lear to find the necessary supplies for their comfort. Edgar, still disguised as Tom o' Bedlam, continues his chatter about the foul fiends that are plaguing him. Alluding to Chaucer's "Monk's Tale," he says that Frateretto tells him "Nero is an angler in the lake of darkness." He implores the Fool to pray and beware of the "foul fiend." The Fool continues his light-hearted humor, asking whether a madman is a yeoman or a gentleman, to which Lear quickly replies, "A king, a king."

Breaking into the middle of the Fool's continued jesting, the King suddenly decides to conduct a mock trial. Edgar will be his "learned justicer" and his wise Fool will assist him. He appoints Kent as one of the judges. His daughters, Goneril and Regan, are the "she-foxes" who are brought to trial, taking the form of joint stools.

Kent urges Lear to lie down and rest, but Lear ignores his pleas and decides that Goneril will be the first to be arraigned. Lear testifies that she "kick'd the poor king her father." Turning his thoughts to Regan, he rails at her for the corruption she has brought and censures the "false justicer" for letting her escape. Feeling deep sympathy for the King in his madness, Kent realizes Lear's wits are failing. Edgar also tells us that his tears for the King make his disguise and buffoonery difficult to maintain. Kent finally convinces the King to lie down and rest.

Gloucester enters, asking for Lear but is told by Kent that his "wits are gone." Gloucester instructs Kent to put him in a litter and quickly drive him to Dover because his life is in danger. He warns Kent that within a half hour the King and everyone associated with him will be killed if they stay in this place. Making sure the Fool is not left behind, Kent orders him to help lift his master, who is now asleep.

Left alone, Edgar, again speaking in verse, drops his disguise as Tom o' Bedlam and decides he will disclose his true identity and get involved in the recent events of the kingdom. After seeing the King's suffering, he decides that his pain is light by contrast. He ends by wishing the King a safe escape.

Analysis

Lear's mock trial of his daughters, the "she-foxes," is closely associated with grotesque comedy. Bordering on the absurd, Lear, in his madness, appoints Tom o' Bedlam as his "robed man of justice" which is, of course, a pun on his sole article of clothing, a blanket. The incongruity of the Fool acting as a "yoke-fellow of equity," a legal partner of Tom o' Bedlam, is utterly preposterous. Two joint-stools are set up representing Lear's daughters, the defendants. The Fool immediately mistakes Goneril for a joint-stool and all the while Edgar is muttering about the foul fiend who persecutes him. Goneril has committed the crime of kicking "the poor king her father," and even the household dogs bark at him. Lear has, in his madness, turned his tragedy into an undignified farce, arousing our pity, but not our reverence and awe.

Kent's deep concern for the King's welfare, consistent throughout the scene and the play as a whole, lends dignity to Lear: "O pity! Sir, where is the patience now/ That you so oft have boasted to retain?" Edgar, too, breaks down, almost unable to go on, as he sees the King slip further into madness. Even Lear himself, still seeking for an answer to his tragic situation, wishes to "anatomize Regan" so he can get at the cause of her hard heart. This is only temporary, however, as he quickly turns to Edgar, ready to refashion his garments, and we are back to absurdity again.

This is the last appearance of the Fool in the play. His affinity with Cordelia is noteworthy. When we first meet him, he is yearning for Cordelia who has been banished by the King, and he disappears from the action before she reappears. In Act V, Scene 3, Lear, holding the dead Cordelia in his arms, talks of his poor fool being hanged. There has been much controversy over this passage since the Fool has not been seen in the play since Act III. Some critics say that "Fool" is an affectionate name for Cordelia and others simply admit to confusion. The Fool has acted as Lear's conscience, functioning to disturb him with truths about his erroneous choices regarding the division of his kingdom and the resultant effects they have had on his life. The wise sayings of the Fool have sometimes been disguised as paradoxical truths. Overall, his wisdom and insight have usually been cloaked in riddles and humorous verse bordering on the grotesque.

Edgar's last speech is spoken in verse as he sheds his disguise as Tom o' Bedlam to follow the rumored events between France and England: "Tom away!/ Mark the high noises, and thyself bewray." Edgar's opportunity to share in Lear's suffering has made his own pain seem "light and portable." The next time we see Edgar he will again need to disguise himself as Tom o' Bedlam as he leads his blind father to Dover. The motive for his disguise will no longer be fear of Gloucester but one of love and concern for him instead.

Study Questions

1. Who are the defendants in Lear's mock trial?

2. Who is chosen by Lear as the "justicer" in the mock trial?

3. Why does Lear refer to Edgar as a "robed man of justice"?

4. What is the Fool's position in the mock trial?

5. How does Kent respond to his position as one of the judges?

6. Whom does the King arraign first in the mock trial?

7. What is Goneril's crime in the trial?

8. What does the King wish to do to Regan?

9. What does Gloucester tell Kent to do with the King? Why?

10. What is significant about Edgar's actions at the end of the scene?

Answers

1. Goneril and Regan are the defendants in Lear's mock trial.

2. Lear chooses Edgar, disguised as Tom o' Bedlam, as his "justicer."

3. The blanket Edgar wears is considered a robe by Lear.

4. The Fool is Edgar's "yoke-fellow of equity" or legal partner.

5. Kent feels only pity for the King and says very little.

6. The King arraigns Goneril first.

7. Goneril's crime is kicking "the poor king her father."

8. The King would like to "anatomize Regan" to find the cause of her "hard heart."

9. Gloucester tells Kent to take the King to Dover in a litter. Gloucester is afraid for the King's life.

10. Edgar's pain has become "light and portable" and he feels restored.

Suggested Essay Topics

1. The Fool is considered to be Lear's conscience in the play. Write an essay explaining this concept. In what ways does he represent Lear's conscience? How does he use paradox to bring out truth in the play? What forms do his wisdom usually take? Why are the Fool's methods an effective way of exposing the truth? Use examples from the play to explain your answer.

2. Lear's mock trial reveals the incongruity of his actions as a king. Write an essay explaining the way in which the mock trial is incongruous behavior for a king. How do the supposed legal titles of Edgar and the Fool add to that incongruity? Cite examples from the play to support your argument.

Act III, Scene 7

New Characters:

Servant #1: *Cornwall's servant who stabs him and is fatally wounded by Regan*

Servants #2 and #3: *they follow Gloucester to Dover and soothe his bleeding eyes.*

Summary

Cornwall instructs Goneril to bring Albany a letter containing the news that France's army has landed. He then orders his servants to find the traitor Gloucester and bring him back. Regan wants him hanged immediately, and Goneril calls for his eyes to be plucked out. Assuring them he will take care of things, Cornwall advises Edmund to accompany Goneril since their revengeful act toward his father will not be fit for his eyes. Cornwall asks Goneril to encourage the Duke of Albany to send an answer back as quickly as possible. He bids Goneril and Edmund goodbye, addressing him as "my Lord of Gloucester." Oswald enters with reports that Lear is being conveyed to Dover by the Lord of Gloucester accompanied by about 36 of the King's knights. He has also heard they will all be

under the protection of well-armed friends in Dover. Oswald then prepares the horses for his mistress Goneril, and she and Edmund begin their journey.

Cornwall's servants quickly bring Gloucester back to his castle where he is immediately bound to a chair and cross-examined. Addressing them as guests, Gloucester begs them not to involve him in any foul play. Plucking his beard, Regan calls him an "ingrateful fox" and a "filthy traitor." Gloucester rebukes Regan for her unkind treatment of her host. Continuing their inquiry with harsh invectives against the so-called traitor, Cornwall and Regan question him about the letter from France and about the "lunatic" King. Gloucester admits the King is on his way to Dover where he will be protected from Regan and Goneril's cruel treatment of him. Lashing out at them for leaving Lear out in the storm, Gloucester calls for swift vengeance from heaven to overtake the King's children. In response, Cornwall promptly gouges out one of his eyes. As Gloucester cries for help, Regan coldly prods Cornwall to pluck out the other eye, too. In defense of Gloucester, Cornwall's lifelong servant draws his sword and orders Cornwall to stop tormenting the old Duke. Cornwall is wounded and Regan grabs a sword, stabbing the servant in the back and killing him. Cornwall immediately gouges out Gloucester's other eye. Calling for his son Edmund to "quit this horrid act," Gloucester is told it was Edmund who disclosed his father's act of treason. Invoking the gods to forgive him for his foolishness in trusting Edmund, Gloucester blesses Edgar and hopes he will prosper. Regan orders Gloucester thrust out to "smell/ His way to Dover." As Regan leads her wounded husband by the arm, Cornwall orders the dead servant thrown on the dunghill.

Left alone with Gloucester, two of the servants decide to follow him to Dover with the hope of engaging the help of Tom o' Bedlam to lead the blind Duke. But first they apply a soothing remedy to his bleeding face.

Analysis

In this scene we see the most overt expression of cruelty anywhere in the play, and, perhaps, in all of Shakespeare's works. Cornwall unmercifully gouges out Gloucester's eyes, which is shocking to our human sensibilities and has contributed to the difficulty producers have long had in staging this scene. Some critics have perceived Cornwall's deed as an awe-inspiring act of terror designed to satisfy the human desire for sensationalism in Shakespeare's sixteenth-century theater. This view does not consider, however, the symbolism of the blinding of Gloucester and its relation to the play as a whole. Ironically, it is not until Gloucester has literally suffered the loss of his eyes that he is able to realize how little he saw when he actually had eyes. As soon as his sight is gone, Gloucester immediately sees the villainy of Edmund, who has informed on him. Promptly recognizing his folly regarding Edgar, he asks the gods to forgive him. Stanley Cavell has observed that these three actions take only 20 syllables. Gloucester's "complete acquiescence" to his sudden fate is, according to Cavell, attributed to the Duke's realization that his blindness is a retribution for past deeds, "forcing him to an insight about his life as a whole" (Stanley Cavell, "The Avoidance of Love: A Reading of King Lear, 1987). He has misjudged both of his children and must now pay a heavy price.

It is notable that all of the evil characters in the play, Cornwall, Regan, Goneril, Edmund, and Oswald are gathered together in one place, Gloucester's castle. Ironically, Gloucester has literally been evicted from his own castle where "robber's hands" have taken control. Besides Gloucester, the only characters in this scene with any compassion and human decency are the three servants. Fearless in his valor, one of the servants stands up with his sword against Cornwall's brutality. He pays for his actions with his life which stands in stark contrast to the cruel and unprincipled Cornwall. The other servants also show concern as they care for Gloucester. "I'll never care what wickedness I do,/ If this man comes to good." They apply "flax and whites of eggs," a household remedy for his bleeding eyes, before they guide him to Dover.

On the surface, Gloucester's only crime is in befriending the King. To Cornwall and Regan, however, the King represents a threat to their own power in the kingdom. That threat becomes even more imminent as the armies of France hover along England's shores, ready to restore the kingdom back to its natural order. Although Gloucester is the victim of cruel and barbaric treatment, Cornwall and Regan's actions seem to be indirectly pointed toward the King. Except for his friendship with the King and his followers, Gloucester would pose little threat to them. "And what confederacy have you with the traitors/ Late footed in the kingdom?" asks Cornwall. Regan demands to know "To whose hands you have sent the lunatic king." They associate Gloucester with the King's potential political power. Regan also condemns his age and parenthood by plucking his gray beard and making condescending remarks about his age: "So white, and such a traitor?" They also support and identify with Edmund, who has double-crossed his own father.

Images of sight pervade this scene, moving the action forward. Gloucester echoes Goneril's words in her desire to "pluck out" Gloucester's eyes. As his reason for sending the King to Dover, Gloucester tells Regan he "would not see" her "Pluck out his poor old eyes." Threatening to "see" vengeance done to Lear's children, Gloucester's challenge is met by Cornwall with "See't shalt thou never" as he plucks out the old Duke's eye. Ready for the other eye, he responds to Regan's urging with "If you see vengeance," but is stopped by his servant. As Cornwall's servant dies in defense of Gloucester, he cries out, "My lord, you have one eye left/ To see some mischief on him." As if the servant has given him the cue, Cornwall continues the business at hand. He gouges out the other eye "lest it see more...Out, vile jelly!" Darkness then falls on Gloucester who has, at last, been prevented from seeing the evil so prevalent in this scene. Ironically, his insight improves as he "smells his way to Dover."

Study Questions

1. Who accompanies Goneril on her way to see her husband, the Duke of Albany?

2. What news does Oswald bring to Cornwall and Regan?

3. Why does Cornwall advise Edmund to leave?

4. What happens to Gloucester after the servants bring him back?

5. Where does this scene take place?

6. Why does Gloucester say he took the King to Dover?

7. Who gouges out both of Gloucester's eyes? Who encourages him?

8. Who draws his sword on Cornwall and wounds him?

9. Who kills the servant of Cornwall by stabbing him in the back?

10. Which characters appear to be the only good ones in this scene?

Answers

1. Goneril is accompanied by Edmund.

2. Oswald tells Cornwall and Regan that the King and 36 of his knights are on their way to Dover.

3. Cornwall says that it is not wise for Edmund to observe the revenge they will take upon his traitorous father.

4. Gloucester is bound to a chair and cross-examined.

5. Ironically, the scene takes place in Gloucester's own castle.

6. Gloucester tells Regan he took the King to Dover so she would not pluck out his eyes with her nails.

7. The Duke of Cornwall, Regan's husband, gouges out Gloucester's eyes in his own castle. Regan encourages him.

8. Cornwall's servant draws a sword in defense of Gloucester. He receives a fatal wound for it.

9. Regan stabs the servant in the back and kills him.

10. Besides Gloucester, the servants appear to be the only good characters in this scene. Full of compassion, they are unable to bear the cruel treatment of Gloucester.

Suggested Essay Topics

1. In this scene, we see one of the most shocking expressions of cruelty in all of Shakespeare's plays. Write an essay discussing the purpose it serves. Do you think Shakespeare resorts to sensationalism for the entertainment of the audience? Relate Shakespeare's purpose to the symbolism of sight

in this scene. Use examples from the play to support your argument.

2. This scene portrays the evil characters as they meet at Gloucester's castle. Compare and contrast the "evil" characters with the "good" characters in this scene. What virtues do the good characters possess? What vices do the evil characters portray? Are they entirely evil? Cite examples from the play to explain your answer.

Act IV

Act IV, Scene 1

New Character:

Old Man: *Gloucester's tenant who leads him after he is blinded*

Summary

Alone on the heath, Edgar reasons that things can only improve since fortune has already imposed the very worst on him. Confident in the belief that he has paid his dues and now "Owes nothing" more, he begins on a positive note until he sees Gloucester. Edgar's mood quickly changes as he watches his blinded father led by an old man, a former tenant. Concerned about the old man's safety, Gloucester urges him to leave since the old man can do nothing for him. Troubled about Gloucester's inability to see his way, the old man is persistent. Gloucester tells him he has no way and, therefore, needs no eyes since he "stumbled" when he saw. Lamenting the loss of his "dear son Edgar," Gloucester wishes for a chance to touch him once more. Edgar is soon recognized by the old man as "poor mad Tom." Seeing his blind father has caused Edgar to feel his life is worse than ever. Gloucester recalls meeting a madman and a beggar in last night's storm. He remembers that seeing him brought his son Edgar to mind though they were not yet friends.

Edgar then greets his master and is immediately recognized

by Gloucester as the "naked fellow." The blind Duke orders the man to bring some clothes for Edgar and meet them a mile or two down the road to Dover. Gloucester says he will allow Edgar to lead him to Dover. The man exclaims that Edgar is mad, but Gloucester says it is a sign of the times "when madmen lead the blind." Determined to find the very best apparel for Edgar, the old man leaves.

Edgar is afraid he will be unable to continue his disguise, but he decides he must. He looks sadly into his father's bleeding eyes as he assumes the role of poor Tom who is haunted by the foul fiends. He assures the blind Duke that he knows the way to Dover. Gloucester then entrusts him with his purse as he confirms his belief in a more equitable distribution of wealth so that all men can have a sufficient amount. Gloucester describes a cliff near Dover where he wishes to go. After that he will need poor Tom no more. Edgar takes the blind Duke's arm and the strange pair begin their trek to Dover.

Analysis

In his opening soliloquy, Edgar expresses genuine hope that his situation will now improve since he has seen the worst. He decides the worst can only return to laughter. A reversal of circumstances in which he sees his blinded father immediately changes his perspective, however. He decides that the worst is, after all, a relative condition.

> O Gods! Who is't can say, "I am at the worst"?
> I am worse than e'er I was.
> ....
> And worse I may be yet: the worst is not
> So long as we can say, "This is the worst."

The degree of suffering is relative to our own experience, and, therefore, we can never say "This is the worst." As is the case with Edgar, the characters in the play are repeatedly led to the brink, believing relief from suffering is in sight, but are again thrust into an even more difficult situation. This is particularly true of Lear and Gloucester. Lear's madness continues in subsequent scenes and his suffering does not end even after he meets Cordelia. Gloucester too has suffered the sting of mistaken loyalties, lost his castle and title, and now even his eyes. Metaphorically, he voices his futility: "As flies to wanton boys are we to th' gods." This is, in Edgar's words, not the worst, however, for he still has the image of his "dear son Edgar," and he lives to "see thee (Edgar) in my touch."

As Gloucester meets Edgar in this scene, he remembers a madman and a beggar whom he met in the storm the night before. He refers to Tom o' Bedlam "Which made me think a man a worm." Shakespeare's audience would have been familiar with this concept from the Bible. It appears in Job 25:6. Bildad is speaking to Job regarding man's position relative to God: "How much less man, that is a worm? and the son of man, which is a worm?"

Commentators have often compared the suffering of Lear to the prolonged afflictions of Job. It seems no accident that Biblical imagery, also from the book of Job, is alluded to as Gloucester asks the man to find "some covering for this naked soul." In his worship Job declares, "Naked came I out of my mother's womb, and naked shall I return thither." (Job 1:21) Nakedness in Edgar is akin to "the thing itself" which is "unaccomodated man." It is man stripped of all his illusions. Ironically, it is not until Gloucester has lost his sight that he gains his capacity to feel for poor naked Tom. He orders a covering for his nakedness which would raise him above a mere worm or a common animal.

Gloucester reprimands the "superfluous and lust-dieted man," who has no insight regarding his excesses because he has no feeling for the poor. Advocating equal distribution of wealth, Gloucester's speech echoes Lear's prayer in Act III, Scene 4 when the King prays for the poor, naked wretches without a roof over their heads or food to eat. Before they experienced their own suffering, Lear and Gloucester had both "taken too little care of this." Gloucester himself admits he stumbled when he saw. Shakespeare's audience, anchored in the Christian tradition, would have seen Lear and Gloucester's new concern for the poor as a sign of the beginnings of a moral regeneration that has come about through suffering.

Study Questions

1. Who is leading the blind Duke as the scene opens?

2. Who leads Gloucester to Dover?

3. What is Edgar's mood in his soliloquy?

4. How does Edgar feel when he sees his blind father?

5. What does Gloucester tell the old man to bring for Edgar?

6. How does the old man respond to Gloucester's request for clothes?

7. Why is it difficult for Edgar to keep up his disguise?

8. Why does Gloucester give Edgar his purse?

9. In this scene how does Gloucester feel about the distribution of wealth?

10. Where does Gloucester want Edgar to lead him near Dover?

Answers

1. The old man, a former tenant, leads the blind Gloucester.

2. Edgar, still disguised as Tom o' Bedlam, leads Gloucester to Dover.

3. Edgar feels encouraged, thinking that the worst is over.

4. Edgar feels he is worse than he ever was, now that he sees his blinded father.

5. Gloucester tells the old man to bring Edgar, disguised as poor Tom, some clothes to wear.

6. The old man says he will bring the best apparel that he has.

7. It is difficult for Edgar to look at his father's condition and still keep up his madman's disguise.

8. Gloucester gives Edgar his purse because he trusts him. He is blind and cannot handle his own money.

9. Gloucester feels each person should have enough.

10. Gloucester wants Edgar to lead him to a cliff near Dover.

Suggested Essay Topics

1. In Edgar's soliloquy, he feels that his fortune can only get better because he has seen the worst. Write an essay explain-

ing the concept that things cannot get any worse because they are now at their worst. Why is this idea relative? How does it apply to Edgar? How does it apply to people in general? Cite examples from the play to support your answer.

2. Gloucester states, "I stumbled when I saw." Explicate this passage in the light of Gloucester's renewed insight. Why did his blindness contribute to his moral regeneration? How has his suffering changed him? In what ways has he changed? Draw your examples from the play to support your idea.

Act IV, Scene 2

New Character:

Messenger: *brings news of the death of Cornwall*

Summary

Goneril and Edmund arrive at the Duke of Albany's palace. As Oswald enters, Goneril inquires about Albany and is told he is altogether changed. Puzzled by the Duke's behavior, Oswald reports that Albany smiled when he was told the French had landed, showed annoyance when he heard his wife was coming, and called him a sot when he told him of Gloucester's treason and Edmund's loyalty to the kingdom. Albany's attitude is the direct opposite of Oswald's expectations. Goneril promptly attributes his changed disposition to his cowardice. Afraid that Edmund will not be welcomed by Albany, Goneril advises him to go back to Cornwall and aid him in assembling an army against France. She tells Edmund she will take charge at home, switching roles with her "mild husband" and handing her duties over to him. She assures him that Oswald, her trusty steward, will keep them both abreast of the latest news. She then kisses Edmund, promising that he may find a mistress dispatching his commands. Edmund leaves in high spirits.

Reflecting on his manliness, Goneril refers to Edmund as "Gloucester" and compares him to the fool who "usurps my (bed)." Albany enters, immediately chastising her for what she has done to her father, the King. He tells her she is not "worth the dust which the rude wind/ Blows" in her face. He calls Goneril and Regan "Tigers, not daughters," as he engages in a long diatribe concerning her degenerate and unnatural behavior. Ignoring his anger, she tells him his words are foolish, coming from a "Milk-liver'd man" who pities villains that are justifiably punished before they can do any harm. She tells him France is, at this very moment, ready to invade their military troops while he wastes his time moralizing. Unmoved by the news, Albany tells her she is a devil disguised as a woman, and he finds it difficult to keep from striking her.

A messenger enters with news of the death of the Duke of Cornwall. He informs them that the Duke has been killed by his own lifelong servant who opposed the act of plucking out Gloucester's eyes. He tells them that before the servant died, he wounded Cornwall who has since succumbed to the injuries he received. Overcome with empathy for Gloucester, Albany is promptly convinced that a higher power exists that has avenged Cornwall's crime.

In an aside, Goneril expresses ambivalence about Cornwall's death which would, on the one hand, give her complete power. Regan, being widowed, would, however, have free access to Edmund. The messenger continues the gruesome tale of the blinding of Gloucester. Albany, grateful for Gloucester's kind treatment of the King, calls for revenge.

Analysis

In reference to Goneril's cruel treatment of her father, Albany censures her for the nature in which she holds contempt for her origins. With the use of imagery representing a family tree, he chides Goneril for slivering and disbranching or, in other words, cutting herself off from "her material sap." He tells her that surely such a tree will wither and die. Referring to Lear as "A father, and a gracious aged man," he reminds her of the reverence she owes him. Albany is certain that if the heavens do not show their powers soon to vindicate the good and punish the evil in the kingdom, chaos will be the result.

> It will come
> Humanity must perforce prey on itself,

Like monsters of the deep.

When daughter turns against father and no respect is shown for age or origins, we are left with Edmund's unnatural world where power is bought at any price, even the blinding of one's own father. Conversely, Albany is the proponent of an orderly respect between child and parent where kings are awarded the reverence that is their due. This is not only Albany speaking but Shakespeare as well. Compare the famous speech on degree in *Troilus and Cressida* (Act I, Scene 3).

Take but degree away, untune that string
And hark what discord follows:
....
And the rude son should strike his father dead,
Force should be right, or rather, right and wrong
(Between whose endless jar justice resides)
Should lose their names, and so should justice too!
Then everything include itself in power
Power into will, will into appetite,
And appetite, an universal wolf
(So doubly seconded with will and power),
Must make perforce an universal prey
And last eat up himself.

Shakespeare's sixteenth-century audience understood the natural law of degree. Bestial humanity, only strong in its "vild offenses," could not long endure, for it would "prey on itself,/ Like monsters of the deep" and finally destroy itself. It is already happening with the death of Cornwall which Albany perceives as divine justice for his "nether crimes." When Regan is widowed, Goneril shows signs of jealousy over Edmund which will culminate in the sisters' murder and suicide in Act V.

We last saw Albany in Act I, Scene 4 when Goneril had just stripped the King of 50 of his knights. Albany, in that scene, demonstrated a rather mild-mannered position regarding Goneril's aggressive behavior toward the King. In view of Albany's image so far in the play, Oswald's words describing him as a "man so chang'd" seem entirely credible. In this scene, we see Albany as the new exponent of moral goodness who rails at Goneril for injustices done to her father. Ironically, Goneril, whose evil deeds have just been scrupulously exposed by Albany, still thinks of her husband as a "milk-liver'd man." Albany's forceful denunciation of the unnatural acts committed against Lear and Gloucester, and his determination to avenge the injustices done to them give us hope that their horrible fate will finally be reversed.

Goneril's attraction to Edmund is simply another link in the chain of events leading to her downfall. Edmund is a master of deceit and comes across as a cavalier in the service of his lady. "Yours in the ranks of death," he utters with grace and charm. Through Goneril he sees his opportunity to achieve the luxury and splendor of the political position as Earl of Gloucester that he has relished for so long.

Study Questions

1. Why does Goneril send Edmund away when they arrive at Albany's palace?

2. In what ways has Albany's disposition changed?

3. To what does Goneril attribute Albany's change?

4. What does Albany accuse Goneril of doing?

5. What news does Goneril bring to her husband, Albany?

6. In what way does Goneril compare Edmund with Albany?

7. How does Albany describe Goneril's personality?

8. What important news does a messenger bring to Goneril and Albany?

9. What is Goneril's reaction to Cornwall's death?

10. Why does Albany want revenge?

Answers

1. Goneril sends Edmund back to her sister because she does not think he would be welcomed by the changed Albany.

2. Albany smiles when told the French army has landed, he does not welcome his wife upon her arrival, and calls Oswald a "sot" for telling him of Gloucester's traitorous activities.

3. Goneril feels Albany is cowardly and, therefore, he wishes to avoid the recent events that have taken place in the kingdom.

4. Albany accuses Goneril of cruel treatment of her father, the King.

5. Goneril brings news of the impending invasion by France.

6. Goneril sees Edmund's manliness as superior to Albany's.

7. Albany describes Goneril as a devil disguised in a woman's body.

8. The messenger brings news of the Duke of Cornwall's death.

9. Goneril has mixed feelings about Cornwall's death. She delights in the power she has gained but is afraid that her sister might strike up a new relationship with Edmund.

10. Albany wishes to avenge the recent sufferings of Gloucester, who had his eyes gouged out.

Suggested Essay Topics

1. Albany invokes the heavens to vindicate the good and punish the evil. Write an essay discussing the possible results of Albany's prediction that "Humanity must perforce prey on itself." Explicate the passage, relating it to the views prevalent in Shakespeare's day. What was their view of an orderly society? What did Shakespeare's audience believe was the cause of chaos in society? Cite examples from the play to support your argument.

2. In this scene, Albany is not portrayed as the "milk-liver'd man" Goneril perceives him to be. Contrast his character in previous scenes to the changed Albany in this scene. How does his change lend hope for the future of the other characters in the play as a whole. Use examples from the play to support your answer.

Act IV, Scene 3

New Character:

Gentleman: *brings news to Kent of Cordelia and the King of France*

Summary

This scene takes place in the French encampment near Dover. Explaining the reason for the King of France's sudden departure from the camp, a Gentleman tells Kent that the King was called back to France on urgent business that, in his absence, could prove dangerous to the state. He has left Monsieur La Far, his marshall, in charge while he is away. Kent inquires about the letters he has written to Cordelia concerning Goneril and Regan's cruel treatment of their father. The Gentleman explains that often a tear would trickle down her cheeks as she fought to control her passion while she was reading the letters. He describes her queenly dignity and patience, and the way she covered her tears with smiles. Musing about the contrast between Cordelia and her sisters, Kent wonders how one parent could produce such different offspring. He concludes it is "The stars above us, that govern our conditions."

Kent informs the Gentleman that Lear is in town, but, when in his right mind, has refused to speak to Cordelia out of guilt and shame for what he has done to her. Kent tells of the things that sting the King's mind. He has stripped Cordelia of his blessing, given her rights to her "dog-hearted" sisters, and turned her out to foreigners. His shame detains him from seeing her.

Kent then tells the Gentleman that Albany and Cornwall have raised an army, but he has already heard. Apprising the Gentleman of some secret business, Kent invites him to come with him to see the King to whom the Gentleman will attend until Kent returns.

Analysis

In this scene, Cordelia stands in juxtaposition to Goneril, who in the previous scene, according to her husband, is "not worth the dust which the rude wind/ Blows" in her face. Cordelia, by contrast, is "queen/ Over her passion." This is reminiscent of the first scene in which Cordelia, by calmly telling her father that she loves him "according to my bond," refuses to resort to the flattery in which Goneril engages. We again meet Cordelia in the next scene, 20 scenes after her last appearance. The conversation between Kent and the Gentleman portrays Cordelia as Lear's ideal daughter.

The *First Folio*, published in 1620, does not include this scene. It was, perhaps, thought to be unessential for moving the action along. For the most part, the scene functions to inform. Expounding on the moral goodness of Cordelia, it signals her return to the play in the next scene. The Gentleman discloses the news of the return of the King of France called back to attend to urgent business. This scene also provides information about King Lear's condition and his feelings toward Cordelia since he has arrived in Dover.

In his effort to understand how Lear could have fathered the virtuous and loyal Cordelia and her self-seeking sisters as well, Kent attributes the mystery to the stars. His belief that the stars "govern our conditions" echoes that of Gloucester in Act I, Scene 2. Gloucester blames the "late eclipses of the sun and moon" for all the societal ills in the kingdom. Edmund scoffs at his father and all others who subscribe to the idea that the stars control our destiny: "I should have been that I am, had the maidenl'est star in the firmanent twinkled on my bastardizing." John F. Danby feels that Shakespeare's sympathy is with Edmund: "Edmund is the new man...Edmund is the last great expression in Shakespeare of that side of Renaissance individualism which has made a positive addition to the heritage of the West." Kent and Gloucester embrace the orthodox view which is already becoming old-fashioned in the sixteenth century. Perhaps this is why Edmund's view is more readily understood by people in our modern society.

The Gentleman's description of Cordelia presents an image of the conflicting feelings of simultaneous smiles and tears. Pearls become a metaphor for her tears and diamonds represent her eyes. She is always the literal and symbolic "queen over her passions." The Gentleman, explaining to Kent how "she shook/ The holy water from her heavenly eyes," metaphorically, capitalizes on the effects of alliteration as he draws his divine image of her. In his poetic description of Cordelia, he has made his point. Cordelia represents the "better way" in her love and grief for her lonely and dejected father, the King.

Study Questions

1. Where has the King of France gone?

2. What letters does Kent ask the Gentleman about?

3. What is Cordelia's reaction to Kent's letters about her father?

4. What reason does Kent give for the differences in Lear's daughters?

5. Why does Lear refuse to see his daughter Cordelia?

6. Who will watch over the King in Kent's absence?

7. Is Kent aware that Cornwall has died?

8. What does the "holy water" represent in this scene?

9. Who are the "dog-hearted daughters" whom Kent refers to?

10. Where is Lear in this scene?

Answers

1. The King of France has gone back to France to take care of business that could, in his absence, prove dangerous to the state.

2. Kent asks the Gentleman about the letters written to Cordelia containing news of her father's suffering.

3. Cordelia reacts with sorrow and love for her father.

4. Kent thinks the answer is given in the stars that "govern our conditions."

5. Lear is filled with guilt and shame for what he has done to her, and, therefore, refuses to see her.

6. The Gentleman will watch Lear while Kent is gone.

7. Kent speaks of Albany and Cornwall's powers so we can assume he thinks Cornwall is still alive.

8. The "holy water" is a metaphor for Cordelia's tears.

9. The "dog-hearted daughters" are Goneril and Regan.

10. Lear has been taken to Dover where he will be safe from his older daughters.

Suggested Essay Topics

1. Cordelia is portrayed as a vision of queenly goodness. Write an essay characterizing her in relation to her sister Goneril. Compare the sisters' attitudes toward their father. Why do you think Cordelia has forgiven her father for banishing her? Use examples from the play to support your opinion.

2. King Lear refuses to communicate with Cordelia in this scene. Write an essay explaining the reasons for his attitude. Is the King still angry at Cordelia for refusing to please him with flattering words of love in the first scene of the play? Has he had a change of heart? Explain your answer.

Act IV, Scene 4

New Characters:

Doctor: *Cordelia's physician brought to heal the mad King*

Messenger: *brings news of England's armed troops*

Summary

In the French camp, Cordelia speaks of her mad father who has been seen wandering around in the fields, wearing the weeds that grow among the corn as a crown on his head. She orders the officer to scour every acre of the fields until they find him. She then asks the doctor whether medical knowledge can do anything to heal the King's mind. The doctor assures her that rest, brought about with the aid of medicinal herbs that grow in the countryside, will be an effective treatment to cure the King's madness. Cordelia calls upon the rare healing herbs of the earth to grow as they are watered by her tears. Afraid the King may die, she feels an urgency in her request.

A messenger enters, telling Cordelia that the British powers

will soon invade the French army. Cordelia has officially taken command of the French troops in the absence of her husband. She wants it understood, however, that it is not her own ambition for power that moves her army to fight. She declares that her motive is solely to defend her father's rights so unjustly taken over by Goneril and Regan.

Analysis

After Lear falls asleep in the shelter during the storm, we do not hear from him again for almost 500 lines. His next appearance will be in the countryside near Dover where he meets the blind Gloucester who is led by Edgar. In this scene, Cordelia prepares us for his reappearance by describing his condition, which has steadily declined into madness. Singing loudly, Lear wears a crown made of weeds and flowers that grow in the cultivated fields. The gruesome picture Cordelia paints is a far cry from the image of the King in royal robes that she remembers. In view of this contrast, it is no wonder that she is moved to tears.

The "idle weeds" that the King has shaped into a crown for his head is, ironically, an incongruous symbol of his kingship. Hemlock, immediately associated with Socrates' death, is a poisonous plant with a disagreeable odor, and nettle is an herb with stinging bristles. Cordelia's aversion to this pathetic image of her father promptly leads her to send out an officer to search for him.

Cordelia does not accept the King's fortune as one that is governed by the stars as Kent and Gloucester would, nor does she invoke the gods to free her father of evil spirits. In her grief, she turns to the doctor to heal the King. Stephen Greenblatt has noted that "Lear's madness has no supernatural origin; it is linked, as in Harsnett, to...exposure to the elements, and extreme anguish, and its cure comes at the hands not of an exorcist but of a doctor" (Shakespeare and the Exorcists, 1988, p. 282). Greenblatt attributes this idea to Shakespeare's source, Harsnett's *Declaration of Egregious Popish Impostures* (1603). The doctor prescribes only sedated rest, brought about by medicinal herbs.

> Our foster-nurse of nature is repose,
> The which he lacks; that to provoke in him
> Are many simples operative, whose power

Will close the eye of anguish.

Symbolically, Cordelia's tears are called upon to water the rare herbs that will aid the King in his "repose." If rest is, indeed, the cure for her father's illness, her tears, symbolic of her love, will be a remedy for his distress, allowing him to rest peacefully.

France's invasion of Britain is sanctioned by Cordelia as an act of pity for her father, the King. It is his business that she is transacting. In view of Cordelia's self-assured integrity, there can be no doubt that she is fighting to protect her "ag'd father's right."

Study Questions

1. As Cordelia enters, what has she heard regarding the King?
2. What does Cordelia instruct her officer to do?
3. Who does Cordelia depend on to heal her ailing father?
4. What will the doctor use in his treatment of the King?
5. What kind of treatment does the doctor prescribe?
6. In what way will Cordelia's tears aid the King's treatment?
7. Why is Cordelia anxious to find her father very soon?
8. Why does Cordelia's army invade Britain?
9. What is this scene's main function?
10. What was the King wearing when Cordelia last saw him?

Answers

1. Cordelia has heard that the King is singing loudly and wears a crown of weeds on his head.
2. Cordelia instructs her officer to search for the King until he finds him.
3. Cordelia depends on the Doctor to heal her father.
4. The Doctor will use medicinal herbs to treat the King.
5. The Doctor prescribes sedated rest for the King.
6. Cordelia's tears will water the rare herbs that will remediate her father's distress.

7. She is afraid he will die if he goes on much longer.

8. Cordelia says the French army is there to defend her "ag'd father's right."

9. This scene functions to give us background on the King's condition before he reappears.

10. The King was dressed in his royal regalia when Cordelia was banished in Act I.

Suggested Essay Topics

1. Cordelia does not invoke the gods nor call on the stars to relieve the King's distress. Write an essay contrasting her view to that of Kent and Gloucester in previous scenes. Does she feel the stars "govern our conditions?" Who does she call on for help in curing her father? Cite examples from the play to support your view.

2. Cordelia justifies France's invasion of Britain as an act of love toward her father. Write an essay explaining her attempt to justify the invasion. Is it right for her to invade her homeland? How would Shakespeare's audience have felt about it? Use examples from the play to support your answer.

Act IV, Scene 5

Summary

Back in Gloucester's castle, Oswald informs Regan that Albany, after much fretting ("much ado"), has reluctantly agreed to raise an army against France. He adds that Goneril is a better soldier than her husband, Albany. Oswald has come to deliver Goneril's letter to Edmund. Referring to him as "Lord Edmund," Regan questions the contents of the letter, but Oswald claims he does not know. Expressing regret about letting the blinded Gloucester live, Regan is sure that sympathy for the old man will turn people against them. She thinks Edmund is on a mission to murder his father and, thereby, strengthen their cause.

Oswald is determined to find Edmund, but Regan urges him to go with the troops the next day since the way is dangerous. Oswald apprises her of his duty to his mistress, Goneril. Suspicious of her sister, Regan questions her secrecy, wondering why she is not sending her message by word-of-mouth instead of by a letter. Promising to make it worth his while, she asks Oswald's permission to unseal the letter. Oswald protests, but Regan tells him that she has observed her sister approach Edmund with amorous looks, and she knows Oswald is in Goneril's confidence. Oswald feigns innocence, but Regan confidently reaffirms her belief that he knows the truth. She tells him that she and Edmund have already agreed that she would be a more convenient wife for him than Goneril since she is now a widow. She promises a reward if Oswald will find Edmund and present him with a token from her. She tells Oswald to warn her sister about their conversation concerning Edmund. Promising Oswald a promotion, she asks him to find the blind Gloucester and kill him. He agrees to do what she asks and, in this way, prove what political party he favors.

Analysis

Only a few scenes earlier, Albany predicts what will happen if Regan and Goneril's "vile offenses" are not tamed (Act IV, Scene 2). His prophetic words have come to fruition in this scene where evil is beginning to "prey on itself." In their sinister attempts to satisfy their appetites for power, the sisters have worked well together. They have turned their father out in the storm, stripping him of all dignity and title, and have blinded Gloucester, who stood by the King in his time of need. But now we finally see the evil results of their licentious behavior turn in on themselves. Goneril has already apprised us of her fear of Regan's competition for Edmund's attentions at the time of Cornwall's death. Now Regan makes it clear that, as a widow, she is the logical woman for Edmund's hand in marriage. Edmund is an opportunist who cares for neither of the sisters, but sees them as a means toward his own ends.

Kent, in an earlier scene, has already expressed his opinion of Oswald and has been thrown in the stocks for it. Oswald had, in that case, only done the will of his mistress Goneril who instructed him to be rude to the King. In this scene, we again see Oswald obeying Goneril's commands. Even Regan's bribery does not tempt him to let her unseal Goneril's letter to Edmund. His stoicism in denying any knowledge of Goneril's relationship to Edmund is also reminiscent of his denial in Act II, Scene 2 where he pretends to be a complete stranger to Kent. As a result, Kent abhors him because he "wears no honesty." Oswald is, nevertheless, faithful to the shrewd and manipulative Goneril. Perhaps his loyalty to her is his only redeeming quality, though he is, in fact, loyal to an evil cause.

Goneril, Regan, and Edmund have all aimed their vicious cruelty at their own fathers, making their wickedness seem more atrocious than that of the other evil characters in the play. Regan speaks of Edmund, who has gone out to kill his father as if it is a trifling matter. It is the expedient thing to do in order to assuage "The strength of the enemy." Evil deeds have become second nature to Regan, who stops at nothing to get what she wants. The outcome of the sisters' rivalry over Edmund remains to be seen.

Study Questions

1. Has Albany raised an army to fight France?

2. Who is a better soldier than Albany? Why?

3. What does Regan think Edmund has set out to do?

4. Why does Regan want Gloucester out of the way?

5. Who sent Oswald with a letter for Edmund?

6. Why does Regan want to read Goneril's letter to Edmund?

7. Does Oswald know what the letter contains?

8. According to Regan, what are the obvious signs of Goneril's love for Edmund?

9. What does Regan ask Oswald to do to Gloucester?

10. How does Oswald feel about his instructions to kill Gloucester?

Answers

1. Albany has raised an army, but only with much persuasion.

2. Goneril, Albany's wife, is a better soldier than he because she has ambition for her own power.

3. Regan thinks Edmund plans to murder his father.

4. Regan wants Gloucester killed because sympathy for his blindness will turn people against her.

5. Goneril sent Oswald with a letter for Edmund.

6. Regan wants to read Goneril's letter because she sees her sister as her rival for Edmund's attentions.

7. Oswald probably does not know the contents of the letter.

8. Goneril has been gazing amorously at Edmund.

9. Regan wants Gloucester to be killed.

10. Oswald will do anything as long as he can get a promotion for doing it.

Suggested Essay Topics

1. Regan and Goneril have become involved in a bitter rivalry for Edmund's love. Write an essay explaining the way in which this rivalry is indicative of the evil characters preying on each other. What do you think this rivalry will eventually do to them? Cite examples from the play to support your view.

2. Oswald remains stoic in his encounter with Regan in this scene. Write an essay comparing Oswald in this scene to Oswald in Act II, Scene 2 where he claims to be a stranger to Kent. In what way does his attitude stay the same in both scenes? Why do you think he is considered an evil character in the play? To support your argument, use examples from the play.

Act IV, Scene 6

Summary

Edgar, dressed as a peasant, is supposedly leading the blind Gloucester to the precipice near Dover where the Duke plans to end his life. In an effort to dissuade him, Edgar tries to mislead his father by telling him they are nearing the steep cliff. Though they

are on flat ground, Edgar talks of the sounds of the roaring sea and the ascent of the rising terrain that is leading them to the hill. Gloucester insists the ground is even, but Edgar replies that losing his sight must have affected his other senses.

His father perceives a change in Edgar's improved speech, but Edgar flatly denies it. When they arrive at "the place," Edgar gives a lengthy description of the view below with its people who appear dwarfed from such dizzying heights. Gloucester hands Edgar a purse with a valuable jewel and bids him farewell. In an aside, Edgar explains that his motive for his actions is to cure his father's despair. Before he jumps, Gloucester prays to the "mighty gods" and renounces the world whose afflictions he can no longer bear. He blesses Edgar if he is still alive and then falls to the ground. Edgar then calls out to Gloucester, but he tells him to leave him alone and let him die. Pretending to be a passing bystander who has observed him from the bottom of the precipice, Edgar tells Gloucester his life is a miracle since he has survived a dangerous fall from the high, chalky cliff. Edgar lifts the disappointed Duke to his feet, and asks him about the fiend he had seen with him on top of the hill. Confused, Gloucester replies that he had taken him for a man. Edgar reminds his father that the gods, who deserve our reverence, have miraculously saved his life.

Lear enters, wearing a crown of weeds and flowers on his head and mumbling incoherently. Edgar is stunned at the sight of the mad Lear, and Gloucester promptly recognizes the King's voice. Lear, in his madness, identifies Gloucester as "Goneril with a white beard." Gloucester insists it must be the King. Lear replies, "Ay, every inch a king" and continues a long tirade defending adultery and denouncing cold, chaste women who feign virtue but are Centaurs from the waist down.

Asking Lear whether he recognizes him, the blind Gloucester laments that Lear, in his condition, is a "ruin'd piece of nature." Referring to him as blind Cupid, Lear asks Gloucester how he sees the world without eyes, and he replies that he sees "it feelingly." Lear reasons that he must look with his ears since he is left without eyes. The King again engages in a long diatribe, railing against the official who administers punishment by whipping the whore when he, in fact, should be whipped for using her in that way. He

adds that "Robes and furr'd gowns hide all," as sin is plated with gold, while those wearing rags are quickly brought to justice. Edgar observes that Lear's talk reflects "Reason in madness." Finally calling Gloucester by name, Lear preaches him a sermon on birth when all come to "this great stage of fools."

A Gentleman enters who has been sent by Cordelia to rescue the King and bring him back to her, but the mad Lear runs away from them, challenging them to come after him. The Gentleman informs Edgar that any hour now, Albany's army will be advancing toward the French at Dover.

Gloucester's tone has changed as he calls on the "ever-gentle gods" to keep the evil spirit from tempting him to take his own life. With pity for Gloucester, Edgar takes him by the hand, leading him to a shelter. As Oswald enters, he promptly claims the blind Gloucester as his "prize" that will increase his good fortune. He draws his sword on Gloucester, but Edgar politely interrupts, asking Oswald to let them pass. Oswald challenges the audacity of a poor slave who would defend a traitor. Edgar slays him, and, as he is dying, Oswald requests that Edmund receive the letter he was sent to deliver to him. Edgar reads Goneril's letter to Edmund in which she asks him to murder her husband, Albany, in order to win her hand in marriage. Drums are heard in the distance as Edgar leads his father to lodge with a friend.

Analysis

The subplot and the main plot have been staged in contrapuntal fashion throughout the play so far. Both remaining faithful to their fathers, Edgar, in the subplot, is Cordelia's counterpart in the main plot. Lear's wicked daughters, Goneril and Regan, correspond to Gloucester's evil son, Edmund. Thematically, both plots have dealt with parent-child relationships. In this scene, the two plots are merged in the actions of Lear, Gloucester, and Edgar. The anguish that each father has suffered at the hands of his children, though it is different, runs parallel to the other. Gloucester suffers physical agony while Lear suffers mental torment.

Gloucester's absurd attempt at suicide has set the scene for Lear's equally preposterous image as he enters, bedecked with a crown of weeds and flowers, declaring he is the "King himself." An incongruous and humorous figure for a king, to be sure, but at this point we can only feel pity. Equally incongruous is the image of the blind Gloucester who has been rendered powerless even to accomplish his own suicide: "Is wretchedness depriv'd that benefit,/ To end itself by death?" His ludicrous actions as he falls on the flat ground prepare us for the comic madness of Lear. We are not, however, moved to laughter but only compassion and tears.

It is Edgar who observes that Lear reaches "Reason in madness." Lear reasons that even "a dog's obey'd in office." He has learned profound truths through his suffering: "Robes and furr'd gowns hide all. (Plate sin) with gold," but if that same sin is found on one wearing rags, he will be quickly punished by the law. He has learned the difference between appearance and reality. Ironically, Gloucester must lose his sight before he learns to see. Regarding Edmund's betrayal and Edgar's loyalty, Gloucester himself has already declared previously that "I stumbled when I saw" (Act IV, Scene 1). When Lear wonders how Gloucester can see the way the world goes, he replies, "I see it feelingly." Gloucester has learned to "feel" both literally and emotionally, but Lear adds another dimension. He advises Gloucester to "Look with thine ears." If he listens, Lear says, he will find it difficult to distinguish the "justice" from the "thief."

Lear complains that his daughters "flatter'd me like a dog...To say 'ay' and 'no' to everything that I said! 'Ay' and 'no' too, was no good divinity." In these lines, Shakespeare alludes to the Biblical passage regarding advice against the swearing of oaths. It is found in James 5:12: "...but let your yea be yea; and your nay, nay; lest ye fall into condemnation." Lear now understands the mortality even of the king. He knows he is not "ague proof" as his daughters had led him to believe.

In his short sermon to Gloucester, Lear describes life as a "great stage of fools." When we are born, he says, we come into the world crying. Stanley Cavell notes that "Lear is there feeling like a child, after the rebirth of his senses...and feeling that the world is an unnatural habitat for man" (Stanley Cavell, "The Avoidance of Love: A Reading of King Lear" 1987, p. 250). Lear had been unaware of injustice and the plight of the poor, however, while he was still the

King. He is now being forced into a new level of human sensibility, and he cries out in protest like a newborn baby.

Edgar's disguises change throughout the play as he slowly progresses closer to his own true identity. Tom o' Bedlam serves his purpose as long as he is escaping from his father's wrath. After Gloucester's sight is gone, Edgar leads him to Dover as Poor Tom, fully clothed but still haunted by fiends. It is not until the fiends are gone, and he emerges as a peasant with altered speech that he calls Gloucester "father" for the first time since he fled his castle. Though unrecognized by Gloucester, Edgar refers to him as "father" four times in this scene. It is not until the end of the play, however, that he makes his true identity known to his father.

Lear's speech, in which he denounces women who pretend to be chaste and virtuous but are actually fiends, is reminiscent of his reference to Regan's dead mother in an earlier passage. Regan has just told the King she is glad to see him.

> If thou shouldst not be glad,
> I would divorce me from thy (mother's) tomb,
> Sepulchring an adult'ress
>
> (Act II, Scene 4, ll. 130-32)

The implication is clear. If Regan, too, would turn him away as Goneril has just done, Lear would think they were not his natural daughters.

Kent has, in an earlier scene, denounced Oswald, calling him a coward and declaring that "a tailor made thee" (Act II, Scene 2, l. 55). An opportunist, Oswald sees the blind Gloucester only as a "proclaim'd prize" with a price on his head. Oswald is insulted by the advances of Edgar, a lowly peasant who would dare to protect a villainous traitor. He remains true to his mistress, Goneril, to his dying moment, however, requesting that Edgar deliver her letter to Edmund.

Oswald is nothing but a "serviceable villain" who does his duty, carrying out the vices of his mistress without question. He has, in this case, entrusted the letter to an enemy. In his rigid attempt at being a dutiful steward, he has inadvertently divulged the contents of the letter to Edgar. Ironically, Goneril and Edmund's secret love affair and their plot to murder Albany has been exposed because of Oswald's strict adherence to duty.

Study Questions

1. How is Edgar dressed in this scene?

2. Where is Gloucester standing when Edgar tells him he is at the edge of the cliff?

3. Who does Gloucester think has saved him when he supposedly jumped off the cliff?

4. What does Edgar call Gloucester after he has jumped?

5. How does Gloucester say that he can see without eyes?

6. What is the "great stage of fools"?

7. Who is Oswald's "proclaimed prize"?

8. Who kills Oswald to protect Gloucester?

9. What are Goneril and Edmund plotting against Albany?

10. What is the Gentleman's news to Edgar about the war with France?

Answers

1. Edgar is dressed as a peasant in this scene.

2. Gloucester is standing on flat ground far from the roaring sea.

3. Gloucester thinks that the gods have saved his life.

4. Edgar calls Gloucester father for the first time since his escape from Gloucester's castle when he fled for his life.

5. Gloucester says that he sees "feelingly."

6. The "great stage of fools" is the world that all of us come to when we are born.

7. Oswald sees the blind Gloucester as a prize since Regan has put a price on his head.

8. Edgar kills Oswald to protect Gloucester from being killed.

9. Goneril and Edmund are plotting Albany's death.

10. The Gentleman tells Edgar that Albany's army will arrive to fight the French.

Suggested Essay Topics

1. Through Lear, Shakespeare espouses the theme of appearance versus reality. Analyze Lear's words, "Robes and furr'd gowns hide all" and explain how this entire passage supports the theme. How does the "great image of authority" apply to this theme? Support your opinion with examples from the play.

2. Lear says that we are born into "this great stage of fools." Write an essay explaining the symbolism of these words. What does the cry of the newborn baby represent in this passage? How does it explain Lear's rebirth? Use examples from the play to support your view.

Act IV, Scene 7

Summary

Kent has divulged his true identity to Cordelia though he is still dressed as Caius. With heartfelt gratitude, Cordelia tells Kent she will not live long enough to adequately repay him for what he has done for her father, the King. Kent assures her that acknowledgment of his services is, in fact, an overpayment. She asks him to change his attire so they can put behind them all reminders of the "worser hours" he has spent with the King on the heath. But Kent tells her he is not ready to reveal his identity yet. To do so would cut his purpose short. She promptly concedes, turning to the doctor to inquire about the King. He tells her the King is still asleep. Calling upon the "kind gods," she asks them to cure the "great breach" in his nature and tune up the discord in his life brought about by his children.

The doctor then asks permission to awaken the King, and Cordelia leaves it up to his better judgment. She is assured by the Gentleman that they have dressed her father in fresh garments. Certain that the King will maintain his self-control, the doctor asks Cordelia to stay nearby when her father awakes. Lear is brought in on a chair carried by servants as soft music plays in the background. Cordelia kisses her father with the hope of repairing the harm done to the King by her sisters. With compassion, she gazes at his face,

reflecting on the suffering forced upon him in the storm. She agonizes over his necessity of finding shelter with the swine and lowly rogues.

When the King stirs, Cordelia is the first to speak with him. Thinking he has died, Lear sees her as a "soul in bliss." He imagines being bound to a "wheel of fire," however. Cordelia asks him whether he knows her and he replies that she is a spirit.

Confused, he does not know where he is now, nor where he spent the night. Cordelia asks him for his benediction, but he kneels to her instead. Realizing he is not in his "perfect mind," he begs them not to mock him. Cordelia is overcome with joy when he finally recognizes her as his child. He acknowledges the fact that she does not love him, adding that she has some cause, but her sisters have none. In a forgiving spirit, Cordelia declares she has "no cause." Questioning his whereabouts, Lear asks whether he is in France and is told he is in his own country. Observing that the "great rage is kill'd" in the King, the doctor suggests that he be left alone to avoid the danger of too much exertion.

After the King and his party leave, Kent informs the Gentleman that Cornwall has been slain, and Edmund has stepped in to take his place as the leader of his people. Unaware that he is speaking to the disguised Kent, the Gentleman apprises him of the latest news of Edgar and Kent who are rumored to be in Germany together. Left alone, Kent decides that the upcoming battle will determine his fate.

Analysis

When Lear awakens from his drugged sleep, "the great rage" has died in him, and he enters a world of awareness and insight he has never experienced before. Confused at first, his mind revives the mental sensibility of the suffering mad King. But he soon recognizes his "child Cordelia" and calls her by name. He has gained knowledge through his suffering and admits he is a "very foolish fond old man." There is no longer any need for hypocritical expressions of love from Cordelia as there had been when they last met in the first scene of the play. Through suffering, Lear has cast off that illusory world. L. C. Knights sees the action in this scene as "a moment of truth...the painful knowledge that has been won will reject anything that swerves a hair's breadth from absolute integrity" (L. C. Knights, *Shakespearean Themes*, 1960, p. 115). This truth has been arrived at through Lear's new capacity to feel. Like Gloucester, he now sees the world "feelingly." When he first sees Cordelia, he no longer makes demands on her.

> I know you do not love me, for your sisters
> Have (as I do remember) done me wrong:
> You have some cause, they have not.

Cordelia promptly responds to his unselfish sentiment with "No cause, no cause."

Thinking he has come out of the grave, Lear immediately recognizes Cordelia as "a soul in bliss." He remains hopelessly bound to a "wheel of fire," however. It seems quite clear that the soul that is in bliss would represent one who has gone to his eternal reward, but much controversy has centered around Lear's "wheel of fire," an image of hell. If Lear imagines himself in hell, there would be no souls in bliss. Mary Lascelles points out that Shakespeare uses this image to show that Lear is convinced that what he has done separates him from Cordelia forever (Mary Lascelles, "King Lear and Doomsday," p. 64). Lascelles continues by showing the torture of the wheel as the punishment of pride. This is accomplished through the account of the pains of hell as shown in the Biblical parable of the rich man and Lazarus. In any case, we can assume that the contrasting heaven/hell image puts Lear on a different level than Cordelia. He has been bound to the wheel of pride while she is free of the deceptive, illusory world so characteristic of not only Lear but of Goneril and Regan as well.

Kent's loyalty to the King does not go unnoticed by Cordelia. Her acknowledgment of his services to her father, though important, is not his chief motive for his fidelity. Kent belongs to the generation that reveres not only King Lear but the very office of the king. He serves his master because he believes in the King's authority. When that authority is challenged, as it was by Oswald in an earlier scene (Act I, Scene 4, ll. 79-92), Kent is moved to violent wrath. Oswald, whom Kent abhors, calls him a "grey beard." Kent is no longer a young man, and he realizes it at the end of this scene when he considers that his labors for the King are coming to an end.

My point and period will be thoroughly wrought,
Or well or ill, as this day's battle's fought.

Even if he survives and the powers of good are victorious, he is cognizant of the possibility that this will be his last battle.

Study Questions

1. Why does Kent prefer not to reveal his true identity to anyone except Cordelia?

2. In what way has the King's attire been changed?

3. Why is the King able to sleep so well?

4. How long has it been since Cordelia has seen her father?

5. When Lear awakens, where does he think he has been?

6. Is Lear angry at Cordelia in this scene?

7. How does Cordelia feel when her father finally recognizes her as his daughter?

8. Why does the doctor want Cordelia and the others to leave the King alone after they have spoken with him for a while?

9. What news does the Gentleman tell the disguised Kent about Edgar and Kent?

10. Who has taken the former Duke of Cornwall's place as the leader of the people?

Answers

1. Kent is not ready to reveal his identity because at this point in the play his purpose for the disguise has not been completely fulfilled.

2. The King's clothes have been changed from the ragged attire that he wore in the storm to "fresh garments."

3. The King has been given a drug to help him sleep.

4. Cordelia has not seen her father since she was banished in the first scene of the play.

5. Lear thinks he has been taken him out of the grave.

6. Lear is not angry at Cordelia but tells her she has cause to hate him.

7. Cordelia is overjoyed when her father identifies her as his daughter.

8. The doctor does not want to risk the overexertion of the King.

9. Ironically, the Gentleman tells the disguised Kent that Edgar and Kent are rumored to be residing in Germany.

10. Edmund has taken Cornwall's place after his death.

Suggested Essay Topics

1. Through suffering, King Lear has gained knowledge and insights he did not have before. Write an essay in which you discuss those insights in relation to Cordelia, his daughter. What do Lear's feelings have to do with his new perception of reality? What has happened to his illusory world regarding his role as the king? Cite examples from the play to support your answer.

2. Lear sees himself bound to the "wheel of fire" as he views Cordelia as a "soul in bliss." Write an essay explaining the validity of this incongruous image. How does the image symbolize Lear's condition in life? What is meant by Cordelia's bliss? Give examples from the play to support your opinion.

Act V

Act V, Scenes 1 and 2

Summary

Among the regalia of drum and colors, Regan and Edmund, accompanied by their soldiers, enter the British camp near Dover. Edmund shows concern regarding Albany's absence. He wonders whether Albany has made a firm decision to fight the French in view of their support of King Lear. Regan is sure Albany has met with some misfortune and Edmund agrees. Jealous of her sister, Regan begins to question Edmund about his relationship with her. Edmund swears that he holds only an "honor'd love" for her and that he has never enjoyed her sexual favors. He assures Regan she need not fear that he will become too "familiar" with Goneril.

Albany and Goneril enter with drum, color, and soldiers. At first sight of Regan and Edmund, Goneril, in an aside, declares that she would go as far as to lose the battle rather than relinquish Edmund to her sister. Albany greets Regan and Edmund formally and politely. He informs them that in view of the fact that the King has many followers who have defected to France because of the cruelties suffered under the new rule, the honorable thing to do would be to fight only the imposing army of France. His quarrel is not with the King and his followers. Edmund commends his statement as nobly spoken, and Goneril agrees that domestic strife is "not the question here."

Albany then invites Edmund to join him and his most experienced soldiers in his tent to determine the proceedings of the battle. To prevent her sister from spending time alone with Edmund, Regan insists that she go with her. Just as the entire party leaves, Edgar enters with an urgent letter for Albany. Insisting that Albany read it before he goes into battle, Edgar promptly leaves though Albany coaxes him to stay until he has read the letter.

Left alone, Edmund ponders over his dilemma. He has "sworn his love" to both the sisters and agonizes over which one to "enjoy" without offending the other. He reasons that he cannot take Goneril as long as her husband is alive and finally concludes that he will use Albany for the battle and then allow Goneril to devise a method of getting rid of him. With Albany out of the way, Edmund will be in power, and he decides he will never grant mercy to Lear and Cordelia as Albany intends to do.

In Scene 2, the alarm sounds as Cordelia and the King, marching with drum and colors, accompany the French army across the field between the French and English camps. Edgar leads Gloucester to the shade of a nearby tree where he will be comfortable until Edgar returns. He prays that the "right may thrive," and leaves his father with a blessing. Soon after Edgar leaves, the alarm sounds within and Edgar rushes to his father's rescue, informing him that King Lear has lost the battle, and Cordelia has been captured. Taking him by the hand, he urges Gloucester to flee from danger. Gloucester balks at Edgar's demands, insisting that he wishes to go no further but would rather die in the field. Edgar reminds him that he must continue to endure but be ready for death when it finally comes. Gloucester agrees that this is true.

Analysis

As the scene opens, we are aware of the Duke of Albany's dilemma in fighting Cordelia's army. He is "full of alteration and self-reproving." His decision has become even more crucial after the death of the Duke of Cornwall, for now he is the top official in charge of the state. On the one hand, he does not wish to fight the King and his supporters, but, on the other hand, he must prove his loyalty to Britain. Shakespeare's audience would not have tolerated Britain's defeat at the hands of the French even though it would be

in the best interests of the King and Cordelia. To resolve his dilemma, Albany justifies his actions against the King by rationaliz-
ing it as a separate issue. "For this business,/ It touches us as France
invades our land,/ Not bolds the King." Goneril is quick to agree
that "these domestic and particular broils/ Are not the question
here." He goes into battle with confidence that his cause is just,
and he fully expects to grant mercy to Lear and Cordelia if the
French are defeated.

When Edmund acknowledges the fact that "To both these sisters have I sworn my love" and yet "Neither can be enjoy'd/ If both
remain alive," we can readily see love corrupted to mere lust. Cloaking his deceit in the language of respectability, Edmund speaks to
Regan with phrases like "honor'd love" and "by mine honor,
madam." Always the opportunist, Edmund realizes that whether
he marries Goneril or Regan, he will be the victor. Unwilling to take
chances, he pledges his love to both and, in this way, assures his
future. He is content to use them to further his own ambition.
Goneril is, perhaps, the better choice since she is already plotting
her husband's murder. "Let her who would be rid of him devise/
His speedy taking off." With Albany out of the way, Edmund can
reach his ultimate goal. Unknown to Edmund, however, Edgar ex-
poses the murder plot by delivering Goneril's letter, intended for
Edmund, into Albany's hands. The letter has been found by Edgar
on Oswald's dead body, and its repercussions remain to be seen.

In Scene 2, Edgar's reproof of Gloucester's unwillingness to
continue in the face of further adversity demonstrates a central
idea prevalent in the seventeenth-century Jacobean period. When
Gloucester wishes to die, Edgar admonishes him for his thoughts.

> Men must endure
> Their going hence even as their coming hither,
> Ripeness is all.

In these words, Edgar espouses the belief that one should
maintain a stoical acceptance of the turn of fortune or loss of repu-
tation characterized by an unflinching endurance in the face of
pain. It is essentially a pagan philosophy that Gloucester himself
expresses earlier in the play. "As flies to wanton boys are we to the
gods,/ They kill us for their sport" (Act IV, Scene 1, ll. 36-7). There is
a lack of justice in this fatalistic view where even the gods offer no

comfort in the face of suffering. Of prime importance is the fact that one must accept whatever comes, be that death or suffering, stoically and with no hope of reward. To accept the will of the gods is the one virtue. Edgar taught Gloucester earlier that he must endure and that suicide is opposed to "ripeness." Gloucester has been duped into thinking the ever-gentle gods have saved his life, and he later prays to the gods that he will not be tempted again to "die before you please" (Act IV, Scene 6, l. 218).

Edgar carefully situates Gloucester safely in the shadow of a tree. There is no doubt about his anxiety concerning his father's safety as he urges him to come away with him after the battle has been lost. Edgar's diligent attendance upon his father is constant and loyal after he has been cruelly blinded by Cornwall. But Edgar repeatedly chooses not to reveal himself to Gloucester as his son. In Act IV, Scene 1, he seems to have reached the perfect opportunity to drop his disguise in response to his father's lament, "O dear son Edgar...Might I but live to see thee in my touch,/ I'd say I had eyes again." Gloucester has just had his eyes plucked out, but Edgar remains cruelly silent. It is not until the last act of the play that he reveals his true identity, but it is too late. Too weak to bear the news, Gloucester dies. It is only then that Edgar finally confesses his error: "Never (O fault!) reveal'd myself unto him." To the very end, Edgar is not sure whether his father will actually give him his blessing.

Study Questions

1. Why is Albany concerned about the battle with France?

2. How does Albany finally resolve his dilemma about fighting the French?

3. To which sister has Edmund sworn his love?

4. Who joins Albany in the tent to talk about the upcoming battle with France?

5. Who delivers Goneril's letter to Albany?

6. What information does the letter contain?

7. Why is Goneril the better choice of mate for Edmund?

8. How does Edmund plan to treat Lear and Cordelia if Britain wins the battle with France?

9. Where does Edgar place his father during the battle?

10. What does Edgar tell his father when he does not want to flee to safety after the battle?

Answers

1. Albany is concerned about fighting his own father-in-law, the King.

2. Albany decides that the war with France is a separate issue from the domestic quarrels with Lear and Cordelia.

3. Edmund has sworn his love to both Goneril and Regan.

4. Edmund and the oldest and most experienced officers join Albany in his tent.

5. Edgar delivers Goneril's letter to Albany.

6. The letter, intended for Edmund, contains a plot to kill Goneril's husband, Albany.

7. Goneril plans to kill Albany, which would put Edmund in the top position in the kingdom if he married Goneril.

8. Edmund plans to show no mercy to Lear and Cordelia.

9. Edgar places his blind father safely in the shadow of a tree.

10. Edgar tells him that "Men must endure."

Suggested Essay Topics

1. Edgar states that he has sworn his love to both Goneril and Regan. Write an essay explaining Edmund's motive for his actions concerning the two sisters. Why does Edmund decide to choose Goneril in spite of the fact that Regan is a widow and free to marry? What does Edmund hope to gain from his relationship with Goneril? Give examples from the play to support your view.

2. Albany faces a serious dilemma in Act V, Scene 1. Write an essay explaining Albany's resolution to his conflict. How does

he justify fighting against the King with whom he has no quarrel? What will he do with the King and Cordelia if Britain wins the battle? Cite examples from the play to support your opinion.

Act V, Scene 3

Summary

In military triumph over France, Edmund enters with Lear and Cordelia whom he has taken captive. Cordelia assures the King that they are not the first who have lost their fortunes in spite of good intentions. Her concern is for her father, but he is perfectly content to be confined with Cordelia "like birds i' th' cage." Edmund then instructs his soldiers to take them away to prison where they will be kept until they can be arraigned. He slips the captain a private note, promising him an advancement if he carries out the devious scheme he has outlined for him. The captain quickly agrees to the scheme.

Albany enters with Goneril, Regan, and their soldiers. Formally commending Edmund for his valiant efforts in battle, Albany promptly demands to see the captives that have been taken in the day's combat. Hesitantly, Edmund delays the Duke by telling him he has seen fit to send the King and Cordelia into confinement. He reasons that the King's title and influence could tempt Albany's soldiers to waver in their loyalties and cause them to turn against him. He advises Albany to wait until a more appropriate time and place when the sweat and blood of the battle will no longer be fresh in their minds. They can then settle the question of what will be done with the captives. Albany promptly questions Edmund's audacity in making such major decisions, thereby considering himself an equal to the Duke. Regan immediately speaks up in Edmund's defense, claiming that Edmund had been commissioned to take her place in the battle. Goneril rebukes her sister, maintaining that Edmund has noble qualities by his own merit. The sisters throw insults at each other and an argument ensues.

Regan complains that she is not well which keeps her from airing her full-blown anger. She makes it known, however, that

Edmund is her proposed "lord and master." Goneril objects, but Albany tells her there is nothing she can do to prevent it. As Edmund enters into the argument, Albany promptly arrests him, along with Goneril, on charges of "capital treason." With bitter satire, Albany informs Regan that Edmund is betrothed to Goneril, Albany's own wife, and if Regan wants to marry, she will need to regard him as a possible mate.

Albany calls for the trumpet to sound, challenging any man of quality or degree to declare that Edmund is a traitor. Dropping his glove, Albany is ready to fight in case no man appears at the sound of the third trumpet. Accepting the challenge, Edmund drops his glove in the same fashion, swearing to defend his "truth and honor firmly." In the midst of it all, Regan, who has been poisoned by Goneril, becomes increasingly ill and must be led away.

The first trumpet sounds and the Herald reads the legal document calling for any man in the army of quality or degree to appear, declaring Edmund a traitor. At the sound of the third trumpet, Edgar arrives. In reply to the Herald's questioning, Edgar informs him that his name has been lost but swears he is of noble birth. He testifies that Edmund is his adversary and a false traitor to the gods, his father, and his brother. Calling him a toad-spotted traitor, Edgar lifts his sword, ready for action. Edmund resists Edgar's accusations and challenges him to fight. There is a skirmish and Edmund is immediately wounded. Goneril protests that Edmund has been duped with trickery, but Albany sternly reprimands her, showing her the letter she has written to Edmund in which she plots the Duke's murder. Defiantly, she challenges Albany to arraign her, knowing full well she is immune to the law. She leaves in a fit of anger, and Albany, concerned about her desperate state of mind, sends his soldiers after her. Aware that he is dying, Edmund confesses his guilt to Albany. Turning to Edgar, he forgives him for slaying him if he is, indeed, noble. Edgar then reveals his true identity to Edmund. Agreeing with Edgar that the gods are just, Edmund declares that the wheel has come full circle and he is back where he started.

Upon Albany's request, Edgar relates his "brief tale" of his difficulties with the blind Gloucester, his father. He regrets that only one-half hour ago he revealed himself to Gloucester as his son,

Edgar. The news was too much for his father's already "flaw'd heart" and it "burst smilingly." Edmund urges him to keep talking, but Albany is afraid he can take no more. Edgar apprises them of the whereabouts of the banished Kent and his "piteous tale of Lear" whom he has been serving in the capacity of a slave. The Gentleman enters, crying for help with a bloody knife in his hand. He informs Albany that he found it on the body of his lady Goneril. Before she died, she confessed to the Gentleman that it was she who poisoned Regan, and then she killed herself. With irony, Edmund notes that he was contracted to both of them and now they will all be married in death. Albany orders the Gentleman to bring in the bodies whether dead or alive.

At this moment, Kent enters, requesting to see the King so he might bid him goodnight. Engaged in Edgar's story, Albany has completely forgotten the incarceration of Cordelia and Lear. He questions Edmund, but is interrupted as the bodies of Goneril and Regan are brought in. As Edmund "pants for life," he hurriedly decides to do some good in the world by rescinding his orders against the lives of Lear and Cordelia. He hands Edgar his sword to give to the captain as a token of reprieve, but it is too late. Lear enters in a few minutes with the dead Cordelia in his arms. In his agony, Lear knows she is "dead as earth," but tries to find some life. Horror-stricken, Kent attempts to comfort the King by kneeling to him and identifying himself as Lear's friend, the noble Kent. But Lear shouts back in desperation, calling them all murderers and traitors. The King feels some comfort in the fact that he killed the slave who was hanging Cordelia.

Lear then recognizes Kent but asks about his servant Caius. Kent tells him he is the same man as Caius who has followed the King since the time his fortunes began to decline. Kent informs the King his oldest daughters have died by their own hands (which is only true of Goneril). Lear takes the news without emotion which leads Albany to conclude that he is not in his right mind.

A messenger enters, announcing Edmund's death, but Albany replies simply, "That's but a trifle here." Addressing the "lords and noble friends" who are present, Albany recognizes the King as the "absolute power" for as long as he lives. He grants honor to the virtuous and punishment for his foes.

Lear again cries out that his "poor fool is hang'd." As he gazes on the dead Cordelia's face and lips, he dies. Edgar thinks he has fainted and coaxes him to "look up," but Kent admonishes him to let the King pass. Albany instructs Kent and Edgar to rule the state jointly, but Kent declines the offer. He says he must soon follow his master. Only Edgar is left to restore order in the state.

Analysis

This final scene, the catastrophe, represents the falling action of the play. It winds up the plot and, because it is a tragedy, involves the death of the tragic hero. Today, denouement is a term more commonly used though it is not limited to tragedy. In *King Lear*, it includes the clearing up of mistaken identities and disguises, as in the case of Kent and Edgar. The villain, who is Edmund, is also exposed and brought to justice in the last scene. The reunion of father and child is demonstrated in the main plot through Lear and Cordelia, as they are led away to prison, and in the subplot through Edgar and Gloucester. When Edgar makes himself known to Gloucester, his mixed emotions of joy and grief cause his heart to "burst smilingly." Though father and son are momentarily reunited, the meeting ends tragically with the death of Gloucester. Representing the tragic hero of the subplot, it is essential that Gloucester should die before Lear. Echoing Gloucester's death in the subplot, Lear dies in somewhat the same manner. As Kent implies, the King dies of a broken heart: "Break heart, I prithee break!"

One of the central themes of the play is the education and transformation of Lear. He has gained new insights and knowledge through suffering brought about by his own folly. Humiliated by his older daughters, he has come to realize that their flattery meant nothing, for he found he was not "ague proof." High position was of no use to him in the raging storm. Slowly he has been stripped not only of wealth and power, but of pride and deception. Now all that is left for him are the bare realities. In this scene, as he goes away to prison with Cordelia, they will "sing like birds i' th' cage." Purged of the outward trappings of pride that were once so important to him, he will make up for lost time as he and Cordelia

...laugh

At gilded butterflies, and hear poor rogues
Talk of court news; and we'll talk with them too—
Who loses and who wins; who's in, who's out—
And take upon's the mystery of things
As if we were God's spies;

He now sees himself as a mere impartial observer of the trivial life of the royal court. With new insight he rejects his past life and his past beliefs. L. C. Knights states "For what takes place in *King Lear* we can find no other word than renewal."

The subplot intensifies the theme as it runs parallel to the main plot. Gloucester too begins to see after he is blinded. His lack of insight regarding Edmund's deception has, ironically, cost him his eyes.

Albany's earlier prediction that "Humanity must perforce prey on itself,/ Like monsters of the deep" (IV, 1, I. 48-9) has reached its final climax in this scene. In this reference he pointed to Goneril and Regan's cruel treatment of their father, and his fear that chaos and anarchy would be the result. As Albany anticipated, Goneril and Regan, involved in a love triangle with Edmund, have finally turned their hatred on each other as Goneril poisons Regan and then kills herself. Edmund is stabbed by Edgar because of his traitorous attempt on Albany's life. Edmund is a Shakespearean villain whose wheel has now come full circle, for, as Edgar says, "The gods are just," and Edmund is back where he began.

The "noble Kent" who has served his master, the King, so selflessly throughout the play, is growing old. We are led to believe he will shortly follow the King in death. "I have a journey, sir, shortly to go:/ My master calls me, I must not say no." Devoted to the King, Kent is of a different time when Lear's name was still revered. After the death of Lear, he recognizes that his time will soon come and he is ready. When Kent comes "To bid my king and master aye good night," we can clearly see the symbolism as being that of death, not only Lear's but also his own. This is true particularly in the light of his last speech in the play.

After Lear's death, Kent's comment, "The wonder is he hath endur'd so long," echoes Cordelia's words spoken earlier. She has just heard the account of her father's night in the storm where he was sheltered in a hovel with the common beasts. "Tis wonder that

thy life and wits at once/ Had not concluded all" (IV, 7, l. 40-1). Lear seems to survive the most dire circumstances, and when he finally dies, Edgar, still unbelieving, wants him to "look up."

An understanding of the play must necessarily include an adequate perception of the Elizabethan view of order. Harry Levin, in the Introduction to *The Riverside Shakespeare* describes this divine order.

The age-old conception of a "great chain of being," extending from God through the angels toward mankind and downward to beasts, plants, and inanimate matter, links together all created things.

This idea has been reviewed elsewhere in the text, but it bears repeating in the light of Kent's comment as he sees Lear enter with the dead Cordelia in his arms. "Is this the promis'd end?" Kent asks, and Edgar adds "Or image of that horror?" John Holloway notes that "the king's end is like the end of the world: not the Day of Judgement, but the universal cataclysm which was to precede it" (John Holloway, "King Lear," 1961). For the Elizabethans then, any breakdown in the natural universal order could be a potential for a collapse into world chaos. Their belief that the end of the world was imminent was an integral part of their fears. Though set in pre-Christian Britain, this is, nevertheless, the world of *King Lear*, beginning with Lear's unnatural division of the kingdom and ending with Edgar's almost impossible task of restoring some semblance of order to the "gor'd state."

Study Questions

1. Who has taken Lear and Cordelia captive after the French have lost the battle?

2. Who delivers Goneril's letter, intended for Edmund, to Albany?

3. Who answers the Herald's third trumpet sound?

4. How does Gloucester die?

5. How do Goneril and Regan die?

6. How does Edmund react to being stabbed by Edgar?

7. What have Goneril and Edmund planned to do to Albany?

8. How does Lear feel about going to prison with Cordelia?

9. What becomes of Cordelia in prison?

10. Who is left to rule the kingdom at the end of the play?

Answers

1. Lear and Cordelia have been taken captive by Edmund.

2. Edgar delivers Goneril's letter to Albany.

3. Edgar appears on the call of the third trumpet to expose his half-brother Edmund as a villainous traitor.

4. His heart bursts when Edgar reveals himself as his true son.

5. Goneril poisons Regan and then kills herself with a knife.

6. Edmund forgives Edgar for killing him as long as he proves to be noble.

7. Goneril and Edmund have planned to kill Albany.

8. Lear is happy to be in prison with his long-lost daughter. In prison, they will sing and discuss the matters of the court.

9. Edmund has ordered that she be hanged. The order is rescinded by Edmund, but it is too late.

10. Albany appoints Edgar and Kent. Kent declines and leaves only Edgar to restore the kingdom to order.

Suggested Essay Topics

1. Lear has gained new insights and knowledge through suffering. Write an essay discussing the experiences that have led to Lear's realization that vain deception leads to one's downfall. In what way had he deceived himself? What has been stripped away from Lear by the end of the play? Cite examples from the play to support your argument.

2. Kent is shocked at the death of Cordelia, thinking it might prove to be the "promis'd end." Write an essay explicating this statement. How does it explain the beliefs of the Eliza-

bethans and the way they saw the world? Relate this passage to their attitudes concerning the hierarchy of all beings. Give examples from the play to support your view.

Sample Analytical Paper Topics

The following paper topics are designed to test your understanding of the play as a whole and to analyze important themes
and literary devices. Following each question is a sample outline
to help get you started.

Topic #1

Shakespeare has woven the subplot into the main plot in *King
Lear* to intensify the emotional effect of the tragedy. Write an essay
analyzing the way in which the subplot parallels the main plot.
Discuss the areas of father-child relationships, political power, and
the deaths of the protagonists in the double plot.

Outline

I.   Thesis Statement: The emotional effect is heightened in *King
     Lear* with Shakespeare's use of a subplot that mirrors the fa-
     ther-child relationships, the corruption of political power, and
     the death of the protagonist in the main plot.

II. Parallels of father-child relationships

   A.   Lear's daughter Cordelia parallels Gloucester's son Edgar.

      1.   Both Cordelia and Edgar are loyal to their fathers to
           the end.

      2.   Cordelia is banished and Edgar is forced into hiding.

  B. Lear's daughters Goneril and Regan parallel Gloucester's son Edmund.

      1.   Goneril and Regan flatter Lear just as Edmund deceives Gloucester.

      2.   Both Lear and Gloucester talk of the ingratitude of their children.

  C. Lear and Gloucester are both blind to their children.

      1.   Lear is blind to Cordelia's love and to Goneril and Regan's ulterior motives.

      2.   Gloucester is blind to Edmund's deceit and trickery.

III. Parallels of greed in political power

  A. Goneril and Regan seek political power.

      1.   They strip the King of all his train of followers.

      2.   They reject the King's title and turn him out into the storm.

  B. Edmund has high political aspirations.

      1.   He allows Gloucester to be blinded for his own political gain.

      2.   He usurps Edgar's legitimate title as the future Earl of Gloucester.

  C. Kent and Edgar both lose their nobility.

      1.   The Earl of Kent is banished for his honest defense of Cordelia.

      2.   Edgar loses his claim to nobility through the deceit and trickery of Edmund.

IV. Parallels in the deaths of Lear and Gloucester

  A. Both die in the presence of their loyal children.

      1.   Lear dies with Cordelia in his arms.

      2.   Gloucester dies after Edgar has revealed himself as the Duke's son.

    B.   Lear and Gloucester both die in "extremes of passion."

        1.   Lear dies of a broken heart. "Break heart, I prithee break!"

        2.   Gloucester's "flaw'd heart" bursts of "joy and grief" after his reunion with Edgar.

    C.   Both die with renewed insight.

        1.   Gloucester needs to be blinded before he can see Edmund's deceit and Edgar's loyalty.

        2.   Lear needs to suffer the rejection of his older daughters before he can see Cordelia's loyalty.

        3.   Both find that the loss of title and position humbles them.

V.   Conclusion: The subplot intensifies the emotional impact of the main plot in the areas of child-parent relationships, the corruption of political power, and the death of the protagonist.

Topic #2

Through suffering, King Lear is transformed from an arrogant, dictatorial king and father to a man who realizes the folly of his past life. Write an essay tracing the progress of his transformation as he suffers significant losses in his life.

Outline

I.   Thesis Statement: King Lear is humbled as he suffers the loss of his title as king, is deprived of common shelter from the storm which leads him into madness, and is denied the love and respect of his family that would comfort him in his old age.

II.   Loss of title and position

    A.   Division of the kingdom

        1.   Flattering the King, Goneril and Regan each win half of the kingdom.

2. Dedicated to the truth, Cordelia is banished by the King.

B. Goneril reduces Lear's train by 50 followers.

1. Lear goes to Regan, but she turns him away.

2. Regan and Goneril reduce his train of followers to none.

C. Lear has been turned out of his daughters' houses.

1. Regan and Goneril seek his life.

2. Near Dover, Lear makes a mockery of his title by wearing a crown of weeds on his head.

III. Loss of shelter from the storm

A. Lear wanders bare-headed through the rain, thunder, and lightning.

1. Only his Fool keeps him company, commenting on his folly.

2. In disguise, the banished Kent joins Lear and the Fool.

B. Haunted by the rejection of his daughters

1. He cannot believe his daughters would do this when he "gave them all."

2. In the light of her cruel sisters, Cordelia's image begins to improve.

C. Driven into madness

1. Lear's daughters have brought him to this.

2. Lear feels that Edgar (Tom o' Bedlam) must also have daughters responsible for his madness.

3. Lear wishes to become "unaccomodated man."

D. Lear chides himself for his lack of care for the poor, homeless wretches out in the storm.

IV. Loss of family

A. Lear realizes the folly of trusting Goneril and Regan

1. Lear has succumbed to the flattery of his older daugh-

ters.

    2.   Lear realizes he is not "ague proof."

    3.   Goneril and Regan have stripped him of everything.

B. Lear begins to trust Cordelia

    1.   Lear wants to go to prison with Cordelia where they will be together to mock the courtly vanities of his past life.

    2.   Loss of family has stripped Lear of the sin of pride.

    3.   When Cordelia is hanged in prison, Lear dies of a broken heart.

V.   Conclusion: Lear's transformation has led him from a king and father whose insight has been blinded by his own ego, to a man who has learned to see "feelingly," not only for his daughter Cordelia but also for the poor, homeless wretches out in the storm.

Topic #3

Appearances versus reality is one of the major themes in *King Lear*. Write an essay analyzing this theme in relation to Shakespeare's use of disguise and imagery, and his characterization of both good and evil characters in the play.

Outline

I.   Thesis Statement: In *King Lear*, the theme of appearances versus reality is brought out through the use of physical disguises, the imagery of the poetic drama, and the honesty or deception of the major characters in the play.

II. Appearance versus reality brought out through characterization

A. Evil characters

    1.   Goneril and Regan are characterized as flattering, deceptive daughters, who later turn against Lear.

    2.   Edmund is outwardly well-mannered and proper but

inwardly deceitful and vicious.

3. Oswald is stoic and loyal to his mistress, but inwardly self-seeking.

B. Good characters

1. Cordelia does not flatter her father but shows the depth of her love for him through her loyalty.

2. Hiding from Gloucester, Edgar shows his devotion by caring for him after he loses his sight.

3. Kent, though banished for his honesty, shows his devotion to the King through his constant care after his daughters have deserted him.

4. The Fool brings out the biting truths in the world of the play.

C. Growth of characters

1. Lear grows from a proud, deceitful king to a humble man, caring for none of the illusory trappings that were once so important to him.

2. Gloucester grows from a man who stumbled when he saw to one whose insight improves when he loses his eyes.

III. Appearances versus reality brought out through physical disguises

A. Edgar is disguised as Tom o' Bedlam.

1. He is innocent of the crime for which he is accused.

2. Ironically, he becomes the sole leader of the world at the end of the play.

B. The noble Earl of Kent is disguised as Lear's servant.

1. He has been banished for his honesty in defending Cordelia.

2. Kent is one of the three top leaders at the end, but he declines.

IV. Appearances versus reality brought out through the imagery of the play

    A.   Clothing masks illusions.

        1.   Lear is stripped of his royal robes and appears in a crown of weeds.

        2.   Lear states that "Robes and furr'd gowns hide all."

    B.   Images of sight

        1.   Goneril claims falsely that Lear is "dearer than eyesight."

        2.   Gloucester says, "I stumbled when I saw."

        3.   Begging Edmund to show him Edgar's supposed letter, Gloucester says, "If it be nothing, I shall not need spectacles."

V.   Conclusion: Shakespeare's use of characterization, imagery, and physical disguises in *King Lear* reveals the universal theme of the false world of outward appearances not only in the action of the play but also in the world at large.

SECTION EIGHT

Bibliography

Primary Sources

Shakespeare, William. *The Riverside Shakespeare*, ed. G. Blakemore Evans. Boston: Houghton Mifflin Company, 1974.

The First Folio of Shakespeare, The Norton Facsimile, ed. Charlton Hinman. New York: W. W. Norton and Co., Inc., 1968.

Secondary Sources

Adelman, Janet. ed. *Twentieth Century Interpretations of King Lear*. Englewood Cliffs, New Jersey: Prentice-Hall, Inc., 1978.

Booth, Stephen. *King Lear, Macbeth, Indefinition, and Tragedy*. New Haven: Yale University Press, 1983.

Bradley, A. C. *Shakespearean Tragedy*, New York: St. Martin's Press, Inc., 1992.

Danby, John F. *Shakespeare's Doctrine of Nature*. London: Faber and Faber Ltd., 1951.

Holy Bible, King James Version. New York: Collins' Clear-type Press, 1956.

Kermode, Frank, ed. *Shakespeare: King Lear*. London: The Macmillan Press Ltd., 1992. An invaluable source for seventeenth, eighteenth, and nineteenth century commentary and criticism on *King Lear*, and for twentieth-century studies.

Kernan, Alvin B., ed. *Modern Shakespearean Criticism*. New York: Harcourt, Brace and World, Inc., 1970.

Knights, L. C. *Some Shakespearean Themes*. Stanford, California: Stanford University Press, 1960.

Lovejoy, Arthur O. *The Great Chain of Being*. Cambridge, Massachusetts: Harvard University Press, 1950.

Muir, Kenneth and Wells, Stanley. *Aspects of King Lear*. New York: Cambridge University Press, 1982.